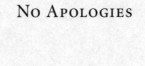

No Apologies

No Apologies

WHY CIVILIZATION DEPENDS ON THE STRENGTH OF MEN

Anthony Esolen

Author of *Out of the Ashes* and *Nostalgia*

REGNERY GATEWAY
Washington, D.C.

Regnery Gateway™ is a trademark of Salem Communications
Holding Corporation
Regnery® is a registered trademark and its colophon is a trademark
of Salem Communications Holding Corporation

Cataloging-in-Publication data on file with the Library of Congress

ISBN: 978-1-68451-234-8
eISBN: 978-1-68451-292-8
Library of Congress Control Number: 2021949635

Published in the United States by
Regnery Gateway, an Imprint of
Regnery Publishing
A Division of Salem Media Group
Washington, D.C.
www.Regnery.com

Manufactured in the United States of America

10 9 8 7 6 5 4 3 2 1

Books are available in quantity for promotional or premium use.
For information on discounts and terms, please visit our website:
www.Regnery.com

Contents

Introduction   vii

CHAPTER ONE
Strength   1

CHAPTER TWO
Agency   27

CHAPTER THREE
The Team   61

CHAPTER FOUR
The Family   99

CHAPTER FIVE
The Vision   131

CHAPTER SIX
The Father in Heaven   161

Notes   185

Index   187

Introduction

I am writing a book that should not have to be written, to return to men a sense of their worth *as men*, and to give to boys the noble aim of manliness, an aim which is their due by right.

Let me set a few scenes. The first is from John Milton.

Adam and the affable angel Raphael have come to the end of their day-long conversation about God and the revolt of Satan in heaven, about the creation of the world, and about man and woman, the noble princes of that world. They speak as friend with friend, intellect to intellect. Adam confesses that he can behold all creation with delight, and without any disturbance in the mind, only in the presence of the beautiful woman

> transported I behold,
> Transported touch; here passion first I felt,
> Commotion strange, in all enjoyments else
> Superior and unmoved, here only weak
> Against the charm of Beauty's powerful glance. (*Paradise Lost*, 8.530–34)

But Eve is no plaything. Milton reminds us throughout the poem that she is royal in her person, her bearing, her speech, and her thoughts. Before her, the most celebrated man or woman among us would appear like a cripple, hunched in mind and soul, ever hiding even from ourselves what we really believe and intend. She seems so "absolute," says Adam, that

> All higher knowledge in her presence falls
> Degraded, Wisdom in discourse with her
> Loses discountenanced, and like folly shows. (551–53)

It is an experience that many a good man has had in the presence of a good woman. Something in her—perhaps a love that can see in an instant what reason requires many steps to attain—seems to sweep argument aside, and even knowledge and wisdom.

Raphael is not one to pull rank, put on airs, or insist upon his dignity. But with "contracted brow" the archangel warns Adam not to give over his place as the head of his household. He recommends to him a just evaluation of his worth:

> Oft-time nothing profits more
> Than self-esteem, grounded on just and right
> Well-managed; of that skill the more thou know'st,
> The more she will acknowledge thee her Head,
> And to realities yield all her shows. (571–75)

Such language is not now to our taste. It is not egalitarian. I will have more to say about true and false notions of human equality quite aside from sex differences (men, from the dynamic groups they commonly form in every culture across the world, have a sense that equality and hierarchy can march shoulder to shoulder). But the question here is not whether what Raphael says is to our taste. The question is whether it is *true*. Would men and women both be happier if men came to a just appraisal of their worth, grounded on powers well managed? Such an appraisal would not boast. It would not swagger. But neither would it cringe or cower, or hang back in exasperated silence. It would be shy to hurt, but it would refuse to lie.

Another scene. Imagine a farmhouse, somewhere in North America, in the 1860s. It is a winter evening, already dark outside, but bright and warm within. Wood is on the fire and oil is in the lamps. The husband and wife have chores to do. She is making a pair of warm trousers for the smallest boy, from scraps cut from a woolen coat her husband has worn out. She is using one of those new Singer sewing machines, the result of a hundred years of invention and improvement. He is sharpening a pruning hook, which he will be using soon on some of the poorer branches of his apple trees. The children are reading a book of Bible stories by the lamplight.

There is a pungent odor in the air, but everyone is used to it. It comes from the oil in the lamps. Thousands of miles away, men are scrambling up the masts to cut the sails as a sudden storm tosses the ship like a cork. They are the bravest and the most blessedly foolish of men, making what fortune they can by pursuing the whale, whose oil they will render in a try-works on the ship itself and then store in hundreds of huge casks. That oil is in the lamps in that home. It was the lubricant also for the various mills that made the sewing machine, the store-bought cloth, the pruning hook, and the press that printed the book. Men commit themselves to years at sea, they fight the storms and the creatures of the deep, they eat hard fare often riddled with weevils, they sleep in bunks without room to stretch, and sometimes they sing, and sometimes they quarrel and curse, and often they die for the oil to light the lamps and make the machines run smooth. The woman at her sewing, the man at his sharpening, and the children musing upon the book depend upon some man up a mainmast, where one false move would cost him his life.

Another scene. You are standing at the edge of a vast sea of grasses, with not a tree in sight. Birds and animals there are, and the buffalo, thousands in a herd to shake the earth, have left many a sign of their passing through. But there are no farms, no roads, no houses, no towns, no barges on the shallow and sluggish rivers, no canals, no mills. Beneath your feet, for many hundreds of miles in all directions, lies some of the richest soil in the world. It is untilled, and except for the natives who hunt the grazing beasts, it feeds no one. In one century, a mere blink in the eye of the life of mankind on earth, this land will be crisscrossed with the most life-giving and life-expanding works of man's labor and intelligence, and it will feed *billions*. Men will make that happen.

It is still so. Look around you. Every road you see was laid by men. Every house, church, every school, every factory, every public building was raised by the hands of men. You eat with a stainless-steel fork; the iron was mined and the carbon was quarried by men. You type a message on your computer; the plastic it is made of came from petroleum dredged out of the earth, often out of earth beneath hundreds of feet of sea water, by men. The electricity that powers your computer—where did it come from? Perhaps from an enormous turbine whirled about by countless tons of water, on a great river dammed up by men, or from a power plant burning coal, harvested out of the earth, with considerable risk, by men. The whole of your civilization rests upon the shoulders of men who have done work that most people will not do—and that the physically weaker sex could not have done. There is more to it than physical force, as I will show. The differences between the sexes, which are manifold and profound, are all related in some way to that one, the easiest to see and the hardest to deny. But there is at least that, and it alone would be decisive.

As I said, I should not have to write these words. I do so because it is a crime against manhood and the truth that young men should never in their lives hear such a thing. I do not want to encourage pride, the sin. But a just self-esteem is not pride. And it is high time that men be reminded not only that they have powers *as men*, but also that those powers were given them to be used for the common good—for everyone, men and women and children all.

In the course of my discussion, I will sometimes have to compare men with women, and, because I am defending men here, it will appear that I am disparaging women. I am doing nothing of the sort. Every strength in one respect, as I will often have cause to say, is a shortcoming in another respect. If men are more aggressive than women are, they are also more violent. The brawler, the burglar, the mugger, the rapist, and the murderer are almost always going to be male. If men are more powerfully built than women are, they are also more likely to break down suddenly with heart disease. If women are more sensitive than men are—more empathetic—they are also more likely to know just the right little thing to say or do to make people miserable.

Men and women are made for one another. I believe it, because it is in front of my nose, and I will not let any ideology compel me to pretend that I do not see what is right there to see. But if that is so, then we cannot corrupt one sex without corrupting the other. Male and female stand and fall together. If men fall into a bad way, women will be soon to follow, and vice versa. When feminists say, "A woman needs a man as a fish needs a bicycle," they not only engage in a blithering display of reality-denial—because where do all the things come from that make up the comfortable world they take for granted, including that bicycle? (And no man would say the like about women.) That is bad enough, but the feminists, at one stroke, are also admitting to a colossal failure without seeing it. They are admitting to lovelessness and ingratitude. If you want to lead well, you have to love those you lead and want to give them good things. To suggest that you do not need half of the human race is to confess that you do not love them, you are not interested in their welfare, and therefore you will not or cannot represent them in politics or further their interests in business and education.

One final point. A grown man is big enough and strong enough to roll his eyes at the falsehoods about his sex that the world tries to press upon him. But boys are not. Boys are vulnerable. Think of the phrase *toxic masculinity*. It is an offense against manhood to talk so. You can have bad men, as you can have bad women, but manliness is a virtue, as is womanliness, nor is there anything toxic at all about either the masculine or the feminine, except inasmuch as bad men or bad women make use of their faculties to hurt other people, to spread lies, or to undermine the common good. The word *toxic* here reveals more than the users of it intend.

Who is *toxic*? The word suggests something hidden, secret, sly. Imagine someone sprinkling a bit of strychnine in the soup—not enough to kill, but certainly enough to make the diner sick. That is similar to what is being done to boys in our schools and in mass entertainment. They are told that there is something wrong with them because they are not like girls. They are also told that girls can do all of the physical things they can, and perhaps do them better—an absurd falsehood. Telling boys these things is poisonous, and I daresay it is intended to be so: those who speak this way want the boys to be weaklings, to despise their own sex, to doubt their natural and healthy inclinations. The old misogynistic literature from the days of the first monasteries was meant for grown men who had made a vow of celibacy; it had the specific aim of confirming them in their decision to give up marriage. It was not aimed at every man, still less at women, and not at all at little girls. But *toxic masculinity*? When you can't persuade the men, you go for the little boys confined to the classroom.

Enough.

Chapter One

Strength

"Acquit yourselves like men," says Saint Paul as he bids farewell to the brethren of Corinth (1 Corinthians 16:13).[1] Most of our contemporary translations efface that strong exhortation, reducing it to a general command that is pallid by comparison, such as "Be courageous."[2]

Of course, Paul did not want the women to be cowards, but he was writing in the first instance to his fellow men, the brethren, and his command is directed toward their manhood. The Greek is *andrizeisthe*, which means, literally, "Be men!" He wants them to be filled with a sort of spiritual androgen, to be bold, not to yield to fear or sorrow or doubt or the desire for an easy peace. Saint Jerome translated it well into Latin: *viriliter agite*—again, "Be men!"

It is a mark of our depleted times that when someone uses the word *virile*, he is likely to be referring to sexual potency, in which case a fifteen-year-old boy has the advantage over a fifty-year-old man. But that is absurd. Virility, in the classic sense, has to do with strength and courage and vigor—what we once called *manhood*. Where has it gone?

No doubt the potential for manhood is still among us. It can no more be obliterated than can human nature itself; it runs in the deepest springs of our blood. Can bulls be made to be as placid as cows? Only by early surgery, and even then, the steers are not really like cows. Supposing that we *could* so alter the genetic and physiological reality of the masculine human being, it would mean our end, our death; imagine a great city, rotting at the core, with no one strong enough to shore up the ruins.

The Facts

If we have anything for which to thank the utterly mad "transgender" movement, it is that it has laid bare, for all to see, the relative weakness of the female body by comparison with the male. Rather mediocre male athletes enter the lists against the best of the girls and run away with the trophies. Again, it is a shame that I should have to point out what everyone with eyes once noticed immediately. Men are stronger than women. They are bigger and heavier, and more of their weight, by far, is in muscle and bone. Their larger limbs make their strength easier to put to use, with additional mechanical advantage: think of the long arms of the average baseball pitcher, who stands near to six feet three inches tall.

Indeed, if you look up the all-time track records for *high school boys in the United States* and compare them with the *world records for women*, you will see that the fastest boys in this one nation are faster than all the women in the world. There are two important implications that flow from this fact. Consider, first, that boys can compete against full-grown men in no category of track. If that gap is wide, and it is, the gap between those men and the fastest women is a veritable Grand Canyon. Second, consider that of all sports on land, running is the one that rewards brute strength the least. A skinny man weighing 125 pounds must do 25 percent more work than the woman weighing 100 pounds just to run the same distance in the same time. Put a 25-pound pack on her back, and see what happens. I am making the suggestion in earnest. In real life—let us say that you are running across an open stretch of a battlefield, and you are carrying a rifle and ammunition—you never have the luxury of determining the conditions whereby you will do one necessary thing (traverse a certain distance) while also fulfilling another necessary condition (carry the materials you need to survive).

If we turn to sports that approach more nearly to reality—the reality of war, of hard work, of struggle against the brute weight and resistance of nature—that *softening* of the differences between the male body and the female body is no longer in force. The strongest and fastest women in the world would be pulverized by a men's professional football team. You would not ask the score. You would ask whether the women could stop a single play from scrimmage. You would ask whether the women ended up in the hospital. In fact, the best female athletes in the world would be made into mincemeat by a half-decent high school boys' team. They would be in danger of serious harm, because the boys would be heavier than they are, taller, faster, stronger, and with much more of that quick-surge muscle action that packs power into the shortest impulses. Again, you need not take my word for it, or trust your common sense and your eyes. A few years ago the Australian women's World Cup soccer team was trounced, seven to two, by an under-sixteen boys' team, and a similar thing happened to the American women's team that actually won the World Cup. And that was soccer—a sport in which you hardly get to use your arms, your shoulders, and your chest.

I hear the objection: *But that is just on the average. In reality there is a great deal of overlap. So the fact has no practical consequences.* On

the contrary, the consequences are decisive, and for practical purposes there might as well be no overlap at all.

First, let us think of a task.

You are a farmer, and you want to build a barn. It is not as if you
have free time on your hands. No farmer does. There are always
things to do. So you buy the beams, the plywood, the tar paper, the
shingles, the nails, the bolts and nuts and washers, and so on. Then
you call together a dozen of your neighbors, to get the thing done in
one afternoon. Those neighbors will all be men. The wives can help
best by tending to their own work in the meantime, or by providing
plenty of food and drink for the men and seeing that the children do
not get in the way. It is marginally possible for one of the wives,
maybe of Norwegian stock, near six feet tall, to climb up the scaffolding with a full bag of asphalt shingles over one shoulder while she
steadies herself with her free hand, or to slant a full thick sheet of
plywood in such a way as to not have the wind make a sail of it while
she stands fifteen feet above the ground and waits to hand the sheet
up to one of the men splay-legged above on the skeleton of the roof.
But the marginal possibility poses more than a marginal cost and
more than a marginal danger. You would not have her fifteen-year-
old son do it, and he is stronger than she is. There is simply no point
in her trying.

Such work is not achieved by the marginal. It is achieved by the
great and obvious *normal*. You cannot say, "Let us gather up from all
the corners of our nation the men with the strongest shoulders, so
that we may have a bridge over this river." Nothing is ever built on
those terms. Army platoons are not made up of giants. When the
Germans first looked upon a Roman army, they laughed because the
Romans were short by comparison with themselves. No matter: the
Romans still had muscles on their bones, they were disciplined, and
they were confident, having fought many a battle in the past. Any

task, to be practicable, must be achieved by the strength of teams of ordinary men readily available in sufficient numbers.

You may say that we can make up for the strength of men by increasing the number of women at work on the job. To the extent that that is true of women, it is also true of boys. That is, if two boys can each wheel a hundred pounds of bricks in a wheelbarrow over to the masons, while a man can wheel two hundred pounds of them, we have not really lost anything by hiring the boys, provided that there is room for them to work, that the conditions do not endanger them, that they have the same staying power as the man, and that we pay them half as much. Those are a lot of conditions, and no woman would now put up with the half-pay. But for many purposes, strength is not *additive*, and two half-jobs do not equal a whole job. If a boy swings an axe at an oak tree with half the force of a man, there is no guarantee that it will take him twice as many strokes to cut it down. There is no guarantee that he will be able to cut it down at all. The tree resists; the blade turns; the wood turns to a gummy mass; the boy's hands are blistered and bleed. If a boy's shoulders can apply half the force of a man's using a wrench against a rusted bolt, it is not true that the bolt will take twice as long before it finally lurches free. It probably will not lurch at all.

In the course of all hard physical labor, the ordinary man in good shape will meet some resistance that taxes his strength near to its limit. Every such instance means that job is an impossibility for his teenage son—and therefore, *a fortiori*, for his wife, his sister, and his grown daughter. He will regularly do things that they cannot do, or that they can do only with profitless and danger-posing difficulty.

I have mentioned conditions above. The boys and the women competing for the mile run on a level indoor track enjoy ideal conditions. Insofar as conditions are *not* ideal, they place an additional burden upon the weak, they reward the strong by comparison, and they make it impossible in reality for the weak to accomplish many a task that in theory they could accomplish. Let me give a whimsical example. Many years ago, I was nailing up long planks of shiplap to the unfinished ceiling of the third floor to our house. I did not enjoy ideal conditions. I had no scaffolding, and no ladder that could help with this particular job. It was summer, there was no air conditioning, and the temperature up there would reach 120 degrees in the heat of the day. I weighed myself after one afternoon of work and found that I had lost six pounds of water through sweat—an ordinary occurrence for men who work in quarries.

The planks were sixteen, fourteen, and twelve feet long; mostly sixteen. I laid a sheet of plywood across the roof-joists, lifted a plank to set up there, then did a pull-up to hoist myself. Lying upon and braced against the plywood, I maneuvered the plank into place, holding it secure with one foot fully stretched out while I nailed the other side. Then, turning to the still-free end, I started a couple of nails, but inevitably the long plank would not be entirely straight—another feature of the less than ideal conditions. That meant that it had to be forced into place by main strength to unbend its crookedness from side to side. But I could only use one arm and one shoulder for that, because I had to nail the plank down with the other. Plank after plank, day after day, 2,400 board-feet of the stuff, and many odd cuts and notches to make for the planks that would sit over the joists—with no fancier tools than a circular saw and a jigsaw. My wife literally could not *begin* to do that work, nor my sisters, nor my daughter, nor my mother at the height of her physical strength. The attempt would be too daunting for them to make. It would make no sense. And with a man around, why wouldn't you want him to do it? The job is obviously men's work.

Consider that this work had to be done in stifling heat. A man's heart is twice as big as the woman's, and it fills his blood with much more oxygen; if they're both in reasonably good shape, a man will not flag as quickly as a woman. He sweats much more freely than she does, cooling his body faster. He has a greater margin for loss. Five pounds of water for him are all in a day's work. The same loss would be perilous for her. Sweating off three pounds of water would put her at risk of fainting. Think also of work that has to be done where the footing is precarious. He has reserves of strength for bracing himself; she does not. Think of work pushing against brute matter of inconvenient shape or in inconvenient places: a devilishly round and heavy boulder you want to heave up out of the ground. If you have small hands and slender wrists, most of the strength you do possess will be wasted. To get a grip, you need the leverage of the longer and thicker fingers, the broader hand, the longer arm, the broader and stronger wrist. The slight and tender hand does not twist and wrest that stubborn root; the root strips the hand. The slight and skinny crowbar fails to heave up that wall; the wall bends the crowbar.

Now, I have said that you do not have boys do the work of men—because they cannot—and that teenage boys are going to be stronger than their mothers. This is not a thing that women have direct experience of. They cannot know it in their bones. I am probably too old now to do 100 push-ups (of 180 pounds) without stopping, but I used to do that without breaking a sweat; I used to be able to do 400 without stopping. Until I reach a very advanced age—and these days, that will be close to 80—or unless I am enfeebled by a debilitating disease, I will always be stronger than my daughter. But the boy surpasses his mother in brute strength when he is—what?— ten years old at one extreme, sixteen at the other. It will happen, and he will know it. He will have some memory of being only as strong as she is. She can have no memory of being as strong as he has become. She can only observe it, or imagine it, and in our time the observations are sporadic and the imaginations in this regard rather dull. That is because many men, and almost all women, are rarely if ever near the kinds of work I have been describing.

But even the boy who is still teetering on the brink of puberty, and who is, for a time, only as strong as his older sister, enjoys a tremendous advantage over her, and one that should prompt us to bring him the closer to hard physical labor. That advantage is simply that he is *going to be a man*, and she is not. An eighteen-year-old girl is pressing against the limit of her brute strength; that is why such girls often beat their older sisters in tennis, golf, and gymnastics, when boys at that age are no match for fully grown men. A teenage boy has a wide field for increase, and his sister does not. We can say even more. With every passing year, her body grows less and less boyish and more womanly, so that most of the weight she gains is not in muscle, but in the fat that makes her body round and that prepares her for the needs of pregnancy and nursing a child. Her hips will grow wider, too—a hindrance rather than a help if you want to be a miner or a mason. Those wide hips will make for a visible angle at the knee, if you go from hip to knee and knee to foot, rather like the angle you see at her elbow if she extends her arms with palms turned outward, and that angle at the knee puts a dangerous torque on the ligaments when she runs or lands from a jump. The boy, in contrast, is pretty much built straight up and down. With every passing year his body grows less and less girlish and more and more manly. He grows tall. His bones thicken. His shoulders broaden. His muscles are bigger. He will continue to "fill out," as we say, until around age twenty-five. We can hear the differences between the woman, the teenage boy after puberty, and the man in their voices. The larynx is the one muscle that men and women, boys and girls, exercise all the time. In the tone of those muscular cords, we hear that the boy is already stronger than his mother, but nowhere near the strength of his father. No one can mistake the voice of a teenage boy for the voice of a man.

Nature never meant for women to wrestle hogs or work on pile drivers or hang from the mast of a ship. The man's strength is for the common good, and in particular for the women and the children. It would be a contradiction for women as a group to define their good apart from the children that they alone can bear and that their bodies are directed so profoundly to care for. Every month the woman's body, sometimes with pain and always with loss of blood and some depletion of the iron that helps to enrich the blood with oxygen, undergoes that cycle that is imperative if the race is to survive. Imagine a menstruating woman in the filth of a ship's hold, of a stockyard, or of a swamp on a dredging crew. What advantage is there in subjecting her to those conditions—what gain would accrue to her, to any man she may love, or to the children she has or may have?

You can have your own politics or your own social theories—perhaps. But try as you may—and these days a lot of people are trying very hard—you cannot have your own biology. You cannot have your own physics. That block of stone does not care for democratic or egalitarian ideology; if you cannot apply sufficient force, it will not move. Those germs cannot be persuaded to turn aside—as you may have noticed from recent events. Wishing does not make it so.

Building Up the Bones

If you compare the Saint Bernard dog, heavy and slow of foot, with the Jack Russell Terrier, all bone and muscle in a small package of nervous activity, you can sense that the bodies and the behavior go together. The Saint Bernard is not going to race around the house yapping and perpetually chasing a ball no matter how warm the temperature is. Or consider the differences between a raven and a hummingbird. The raven is long-lived, big, careful, and slow. It flaps about in lazy loops, looking for small animals to snatch up or for carcasses that stay where they are. But the hummingbird's heart races—hundreds of beats per minute; the highest recorded has been 1,260 beats, or 21 *per second*, so fast that the human ear cannot distinguish one beat from another. Then, as we expect, we see the behavior that corresponds to such a body: the thousands of miles that hummingbirds travel, their energetic hovering in mid-air in a forced and strenuous place-holding, their sudden movements like the shots of an arrow, or how the male dives 80 feet at 50 miles an hour to court the female.

Every typical difference between the behaviors of boys and girls can be seen as the natural expression of the forms of their bodies. The boys have more muscle mass and a higher metabolism; *therefore they crave action*, and they grow restive and irritable without it, just as a Border Collie in an apartment would. It is stupid and cruel not to give them plenty of fresh air and freedom for that action. The boys have muscles that are destined to grow stronger than their sisters' muscles, but how do muscles grow strong? By exercise—in other words, by action. Think of football, or wrestling, or playing King of the Hill. Wherever you go in the world, you will find boys doing things that stress the muscles and bruise the bones. A boy who lifts weights is making tiny tears in his muscles—which actually build his muscle mass. Imagine a horde of boys whooping it up as they push one another out of their way up the hill, or pile one upon the other at the top—the sheer animal joy of it is impossible to miss. Why, left to their own devices, do girls not do the same? Because their bodies do not crave it. The needs of the body explain what is otherwise hard to understand, that it feels good not only to tackle your opponent in the open field, but to be tackled, to come down with force against the hard ground, and to get up and do the same all over again, and to feel the great satisfaction of sore muscles and sore bones at night, a good and satisfying tiredness, when sleep is like a big dinner after a hard day of work.

It is important to assert here that this behavior is natural: it is what healthy boys do without needing to be taught. For until our own sad and child-poor time, the games of children were invented by children, supervised by children, and passed along by children from one age to the next without the interference of their parents. When feminists say that boys are *socialized* to behave in these ways, they make three errors at once. First, they posit a dichotomy between nature and society that does violence to the creatures they are observing, since man *is by nature a social animal*, and the societies he forms without ideological deliberation are but his nature writ large. Think of a dog pack. Second, the feminists ignore or deny the biological and physical imperatives, and indeed they show little desire to imagine what it might be like to inhabit a male body, with its vast array of differences from their own. They do not even bother to ask why men seem less bothered by extremes of temperature than they are. Third, they betray their own desire *to compel boys and girls to act against their natures*, to force them, like hothouse plants. Imagine girls left to do what best pleases them, without any ideological compulsion, and without the boys to imitate. Give them a thousand years, and they would not invent football or baseball. Why would they bother? What would be the point? How often have you seen a group of girls alone spontaneously piling up boulders to build a fort? Wouldn't it strike women themselves as unusual? But you don't even notice when boys do it, because it is simply what they do, everywhere. If you see boys at it, and you are a normal man, you feel a surge of strength and desire in your bones, and you want to be a boy again, to do what they are doing.

I will have more to say in a later chapter about team sports and their significance. Here we should just notice what lies in direct view. Boys are relentless *inventors of games*. Give them a ball and something to hit it with, or a rock and something to hit with the rock, and the boys will come up with a game complete with rules, a game that presses them to their limits of strength and speed and skill. You will see them *losing themselves* in the game in a blissful forgetfulness of the strains of life, a forgetfulness that is like joy. We are not talking about a patriarchal society imposing something on them; it is just as likely that the games flow from the boys to their busier and more serious fathers. It is hard to imagine that Inuit men had the time on their hands to invent hockey. But whether the games came from the men and were passed along to their sons, or came from the boys and were passed along to the men, the games are in concord with the male body and its drives and with the kinds of work that, by and large, only grown men can do.

Look at the young bucks butting at each other with their antlers. They are happily obeying an imperative of their nature, building them-selves up in protective aggressiveness, courage, and strength—and hardening the antlers in the process. The females look on, because after all the males must compete for their attention. The female's strategy is conservative. She cannot afford a weakling. She wants her offspring to survive. Therefore she seeks the strong.

It used to be said that women could not resist a man in uniform. What is attractive about that? That man is at the peak of his physical condition for his age, and his strength is ordered toward the common good in obvious ways. He has built up the muscles by hard work and hard play, and the discipline necessary for protecting his country in time of war. In the sports of the original ancient Greek Olympics—boxing, wrestling, horse racing, running, throwing the discus and the javelin—the men both rested from and prepared for war. But the enemy a man fights is not always the man from the tribe beyond the river. Sometimes it is the hard earth to be broken and sowed. It may be the river to be dammed for power and fresh water. It may be the bitter winter, the snow and ice to be overcome, or even put to use, as men with ice-saws used to cut great blocks out of the frozen lake to pack in sawdust in the ice house, so that they, their wives, and their children could enjoy cold drinks or ice cream six months later—and have ice to keep their bodies cool if the fever should come through again. In that case, ice in July might be the difference between life and death. Men fight, or their people die. And men grow strong by resistance.

Inner Strength

Of the moral strength of women, expressed most powerfully in patient endurance and unshakable loyalty to the people they love, the great poets with their insight into human nature have much to show us: the faithful and clever Penelope growing gray as she waits for Odysseus to return; Emilia not fooled by the lies of her wicked husband Iago, standing up for her mistress Desdemona, even in the face of death; Hermione standing up for her innocence, preserving herself alive for sixteen years; Kristin the daughter of Lavrans keeping her large household and farm together with intelligence and an iron will while her husband Erlend goes astray; Joan of Arc at the stake; and Mary beneath the cross. Still, there is a masculine strength of character that has met with contempt in our time. Let me explain.

Return to the boys on the ballfield. There is a close call at first base. The batter is ruled out. He has already been frustrated—he has struck out twice, and his team is losing. At this point he can do several antisocial and unhelpful things. He can make an angry scene, arguing that he was safe even though he knows better. He can kick the dog and quit. He can start crying. In all three cases, he would be permitting his passions, his feelings, to dominate over his reason and his duty to seek the common good, which in this case is the good of the game. But he has learned *not to cry*.

If someone says that it is his *society* that teaches him so, my first reply is to ask why every society in the world has taught boys this same thing. We have direct observations or recorded testimonies from more than 1,500 human cultures, each of them independent of a majority of the others. What are the odds that in this matter they would all do the same out of random chance? Shouldn't they vary as much in this as they do in the *words* they use for "boy" and "girl"? But they all do the same thing—training boys, in particular, to control their emotions—because it is as natural for them to do it as it is for human beings everywhere to signal their pleasure by smiling. We recognize immediately what the smile means. We recognize immediately boys at their complicated games, even when we do not know what the rules are. That does not surprise us. But it would furrow our brows if we saw the boys crying over a close play and breaking up the game over it.

My second reply is to ask people to consider carefully what the boys are doing. For the game to take place at all, *personal feelings* must be kept in check. Such feelings get in the way. You need to fight a battle. You need to throw a bridge across that dangerous ravine. You need to go down into the earth to get the iron ore. You need to plane those beams, and your saw needs sharpening. Your fields are getting pelted with hail, and you need to save as much corn as you can. You have strong passions, but you must either set them aside for later or bend them toward the productive task, channeling them, making them all the stronger for being channeled. You must deny yourself, and you grow by the self-denial.

When boys are told that they should let themselves cry—not just in the extraordinary situations that justify male weeping, such as grief for close kin—they are not really (whatever the psychologists and our psychologized world may tell us) being given leave to feel emotions that they would otherwise prevent themselves from feeling.

They are sapped. They are being given leave *not to experience what they otherwise might experience*: conquest over passion, with its own passion too—the confident enjoyment of victory. Go to the most dysfunctional regions of our society, and you will behold boys and men who express their feelings quite freely: feelings of wrath, vengeance, lust, cruelty, delight in destruction. Before we tell men that they should express their feelings all the time, we might ask first what those feelings are likely to be.

We should also notice that in a time of danger or trouble, it is quite valuable to have someone near who can think with perfect coldness, as if nothing mattered to him but the thing to be done. "Let's roll," said Todd Beamer after he had prayed the Twenty-Third Psalm with a telephone operator, and then he and his fellows ambushed the men who wanted to fly the airplane into the White House or the Capitol, bringing it down to harmless destruction in the farmlands of western Pennsylvania. He had called the operator, Lisa Jefferson, because he wanted to spare his wife the immediate shock, as she was expecting a child. Note both the fineness of his sensitivity and the fact that he denied himself the comfort of speaking to his wife, *for her sake*. We know that even when weeping, or shivering with fear, or groaning with pain may be perfectly understandable, it may not always be useful—and it may not be the best way of showing charity toward others. The man who does not weep in a crisis is not saying to himself, "Behold how strong I am." He is compelling himself to separate one feeling from another, the feeling that here, right now, will hurt our chances or will impose a burden on other people, and from the feeling that almost has no name, that fierce desire to have the right thing done against all odds and in the teeth of disaster.

I have heard it said that the notion that men must set aside their grief or fear in order to get a job done is a stale relic of Victorian

England, when British men were supposed to keep that upper lip stiff in times of trouble and not betray a single weakness. That is supposed to harm boys who are told that they are not supposed to cry. The problem with this claim is that manhood in every culture contradicts it. Let us go to ancient Rome, for example. The scene is Carthage, and the hero Aeneas has been instructed by the gods to leave and go forth to Italy, regardless of his feelings. He does not want to go. Dido, the queen of the newly founded city, has fallen madly in love with him, and they have been living, somewhat scandalously, as man and wife. Aeneas has gone so far as to supervise the Carthaginian building projects. He is weary of wandering. His own home, Troy, has been burnt to the ground. Why shouldn't he stay where he's comfortable? But Mercury reminds him of his fatherly duty:

> What hope do you hold to, dozing away in Libya?
> If you are not moved by the glory of things to come,
> Or your own honor in such a mighty work,
> Look to your rising son Ascanius, look
> To the hope of Iulus your heir, for the land of Rome
> And Italy's realm are his by right. (*Aeneid*, 4.271–76)[3]

And that is all Aeneas needs to hear. He does not want to hear it, but what a man wants and what a man must do are seldom the same.

So he orders his men to get the ships ready, while he tries to find a way to tell Dido that he is leaving. She, however, with a woman's quick sense, sees it first and accuses him bitterly, appealing to their "marriage," to his having exposed her to the anger of a nearby enemy who had courted her, and to her generous treatment of him and his homeless Trojans. Please, please, she says, do not leave me! At least if there were some little child of theirs that would remind her of him, that would be some consolation. She is utterly crushed.

Aeneas is moved, but he cannot bend—he must not bend:

> But, warned by Jove, he did not move his eyes;
> Leaned hard on the care in his heart, and kept it down.
> (*Aeneid*, 4.271–76)

And when the queen's sister Anna tries to move him time and again with many tears, he remains steadfast. The simile the poet uses suggests *both* intense feeling *and a strong will to master the feeling*, to keep it from altering what he intends to do:

> But as the winds from the Alps in a wrestling fury
> Rage here and there to rip up by the roots
> A tough and hearty oak tree strong in age:
> The trunk shakes, and the leaves lie strewn on the ground,
> But the oak holds to the rock, and lifts his crown
> As high to heaven as the roots reach down to Hades;
> So did the hero, assailed by a storm of cries
> From here, there, feel their force in his large heart;
> But his mind held fast, no matter the rain of tears.
> (*Aeneid*, 4.441–49)

Aeneas, we see, must give up his last good chance for happiness in life, so that others, his descendants, especially his beloved son Ascanius, may prosper. Regrets are of no consequence.

But that was the stoic Roman, you might say. Well then, let us go behind the stoic. Here is Odysseus, in that great poem composed hundreds of years before Zeno ever preached his manly philosophy of self-denial from the Stoa. Odysseus and his men are on an island. They are desperately hungry. They have been catching some fish and small game birds, but it is not enough. Meanwhile, plenty of oxen browse the hills, but they belong to the sun god Helios, and the men have been warned not to touch them. But when Odysseus leaves their camp to pray to the gods for mercy, Eurylochus, who has long complained bitterly about his captain's stubbornness, counsels the other men to kill some of the cattle and eat rather than die of hunger, saying that even if the gods should plunge their ship beneath the sea,

> I would rather at once go down with a gulp of the wave,
> Than wither my age away on a desert island.
> (*Odyssey*, 12.359–60)

That may sound brave, but it is not. The poet Homer presents it as the counsel of weakness. The men give in. To suffer much for a right cause is the mark of the *aner*, the real *man*, as Homer calls Odysseus in the opening invocation of the poem. The rest of the sailors from Ithaca are *nepioi, ninnies, mere silly boys*, because they ate the cattle of Helios Hyperion.

Odysseus is not callous. Quite the contrary. He feels deeply; his name suggests strife and suffering, and the telltale scar on his body is, fittingly enough, from a wound he got when he was a boy hunting the wild boar with his grandfather and his uncles. We see that while other men, such as the 108 self-indulgent suitors who have descended upon his estate back home in Ithaca, seek their pleasure first and do not want to listen to any stories of sadness, Odysseus holds pleasure at bay; he confronts life directly. He knows he will be tempted to weep when he asks the loyal swineherd Eumaeus about the old dog Argos— "Flash" (the name suggests both light and speed)—lying devoured by fleas on the dunghill as they approach the house. For Flash is the first creature in Ithaca to recognize the beggar-king, and he whimpers a little and tries to wag his tail. But Eumaeus tells how the dog was always the first in the pack to trail the game and never lost the scent, but now the servants neglect him, because that is what you get when the master of a household is gone. Odysseus sheds a tear, but he does not let Eumaeus see it, and he wipes it away. It is not the time for tears, even after

> the dark fate of death took hold of Flash,
> When he had seen Odysseus, after twenty years.
> (*Odyssey*, 12.350–51)

That is Homeric Greece and imperial Rome, you may say. Sure, this is hardly the universal rule. But where can we go then to find a culture in which the men weep freely and loudly while the women are silent and hold to their public purposes? Not to India, where the prince Gautama (the Buddha) sat for seven days or seven weeks under the Bo tree, eating nothing, in a trance contemplating the many miseries that afflict mankind—and when the evil god Mara brought forth his daughters decked in all the beauty of the world to tempt him, to move him from his path, the prince held fast, and looked upon them with a sort of kindly indifference. Can we go to China, where, when the master Confucius was asked to describe the perfect man, he did so in terms of calm self-restraint? The perfect man is one who, "when he sees a chance of gain, stops to think whether to pursue it would be right; when he sees that his prince is in danger, is ready to lay down his life; when the fulfillment of an old promise is exacted, stands by what he said long ago." How do you recognize the good son? When his father dies and the three required years of mourning follow, the good son runs the household exactly as it had been run in his father's life. He obeys the sacred custom, and he does not permit the grief to master him.

How about the American Indians? "My grandson," says the old woman in a Native American tale, "you must never go hunting; all your people were killed while out hunting. I don't want you to hunt; I don't want you to be killed." But the boy stands firm. "I don't want to be killed, my grandmother, but I don't like to stay around the house all the time. I want to find food and bring it home," he says, affirming one of the fundamental masculine directives, that of conquest for the sake of the people he loves. "I want, besides, to see where my people were killed. I want to see the place where they died; I want to look at the person who killed them." The grandmother continues to beg, but he holds to his intention, and the grandmother weeps in the morning when he leaves. He does meet the wicked killer Klakherrit, but he does not fall for the vicious man's trick—which is to play on his victims' pity, begging them to pull a splinter out of his foot, and cutting off their heads while they are so occupied. The boy returns home, and the next morning he calmly places a blue and a white stone before his grandmother, saying that if she sees black blood on the blue stone, she will know that he has been killed, but if she sees red blood on the white stone, she will know that he has killed Klakherrit. Again the woman weeps, but the boy goes on his way—and slays not only Klakherrit, but all his wicked people too, except for one woman who manages to escape.

Can we go to pagan Ireland? Fin the son of Cool and his sons, Oscar and Oisin, are defending their country against the onslaught of Daire Donn, High King of the Great World. When Oisin's enemy is getting the better of him, backing him up against the sea, Fin sends to him a poet—a poet!—to remind him of his courage and strength. "Now is the time to prove your valor and greatness, Oisin," says the poet. "You never went to any place but a king's daughter, or a high beauty, fell in love with you. Many are looking this day at you; and now is your time to show your bravery." His fear and worry fall away, and Oisin grows in fury, till he cuts off his enemy's head.

Or pagan England? The poet of *The Wanderer*, with laconic understatement, describes what a real man must not be:

> The wise man knows how to wait:
> not too hot in his heart, or hasty of speech,
> not too weak in war, or wild in his thoughts,
> not too fearful, or too giddy, or greedy for treasure,
> nor eager to vaunt ere he knows how to act. (65–69)

Or we may turn to the poet of *The Battle of Maldon*, two hundred years later, telling us what Byrhtwold says when his lord is dead in the field and all is lost:

> Our hearts must be the keener, and the harder our will,
> all our courage the more as our might is the less.
> Here lies our captain cut down to the earth,
> good man, on the field. May he mourn forever
> who would think to flee from this fight-play.
> My soul is right glad, and I seek not to leave,
> but at the side of my lord, by that man beloved,
> I shall lay me down in death this day. (312–19)

Again, what we see is not a cold heart, not callousness, but the compelling demands of duty and the bonds of friendship overmastering any feeling of fear or despair. Let our sons be brought up with such songs in their hearts.

The Unsafe Space

In every case I have noted, what the man seeks is safety for *others*, at the cost of safety for himself. And that pleases him well, because he finds safety to be smothering and unproductive. Consider the call for "safe spaces" on our college campuses. It is unimaginable that men, by themselves, would call for such a thing; it would be like asking for someone to amputate one of his limbs. When Saint Paul demands fidelity, it is as opposed to safety and ease. Recall what he says to the well-fed and rather smug Corinthians, reproaching those who make light of his testimony:

> Are they ministers of Christ? (I speak as a fool) I am more; in labors more abundant, in stripes above measure, in prisons more frequent, in deaths oft. Of the Jews five times I received forty stripes save one. Thrice was I beaten with rods, once was I stoned, thrice I suffered shipwreck, a night and a day have I been in the deep; in journeyings often, in perils of waters, in perils of robbers, in perils by mine own countrymen, in perils by the heathen, in perils in the city, in perils in the wilderness, in perils in the sea, in perils among false brethren; in weariness and painfulness, in watchings often, in hunger and thirst, in fastings often, in cold and nakedness. Besides those things that are without, that which cometh upon me daily, the care of all the churches. (2 Corinthians 11:23–28)

Paul is not boasting of physical prowess. In fact, he says, repeating others' claims, that "his bodily presence is weak, and his speech contemptible" (2 Corinthians 10:10). The point is that he is a mighty contender for the truth and has gone forth into danger, with martyrdom following at his heels. "I have fought a good fight," he writes to his disciple, the young bishop Timothy, "I have finished my course, I have kept the faith" (2 Timothy 4:7). The Greek here is instructive: *ton kalon agon egonismai*. Paul has gone forth into the arena. The

Greek *agon* is a struggle, a contest while the world is watching. Think of the contenders in a wrestling match during the Pythian games at Delphi. But Paul's opponents have been not simply hulks with big arms and legs. As he says to the church at Ephesus, "We wrestle not against flesh and blood, but against principalities, against powers, against the rulers of the darkness of this world, against spiritual wickedness in high places" (Ephesians 6:12). In such a case, we dare not permit our own uneasy feelings, or our often legitimate concern for the feelings of others, to assume priority over the truth. We must not let what is called tolerance or even love—but what is often really cowardice and indifference to the true good of our fellow men—to cause us to duck out of the *agon*, or to throw the fight.

If Paul was thinking in Hebrew and writing in Greek, as is quite possible, the words *ha-milchamah ha-tovah nilchamathi* may have come into his mind: *the good battle have I battled*. In which case he would not have been thinking of a Greek arena and a competition, but of a Hebrew battlefield and a war.

But in the end, is not the unsafe space a free and freedom-making thing? Safety can smother. When the pilgrim Dante reaches the sphere of the fixed stars in Paradise, he meets Saint Peter, who does not pat him on the back or give him a baby bottle to suck. Peter assumes the role of the questioner in a medieval disputation; indeed, he plays the *diabolus*, the "devil's advocate," to see how sharp Dante is and to determine whether he knows what faith is, how to justify his faith, and what his faith affirms. Beatrice tells Peter that Dante is ready for the test, and Dante prepares himself for it:

> A bachelor arms himself and will not speak
> until the master gives the proposition,
> not to decide it but to show forth proof;
> So while she spoke I mustered every reason,

ready in arms for such a questioner
and such a declaration. (*Paradiso* 24:46–51)

Dante's language is military: *s'arma* he says of the man contend-
ing for his degree, and *m'armava* he says of himself. He anticipates
the test not in fear but in expectant confidence and with a gladness
that he should be tried to the utmost.

We Americans, and maybe the whole rest of the exhausted Western world, are now in a strange place. Iron niceness rules the land.
Not moral virtue, but niceness—a soft and fluffy cover for vindictive-
ness, resentment, and hatred. In which place does a man now feel
most comfortable speaking his mind, a university classroom, or a
bar? At work, even if his work is dedicated to seeking the truth—or
at a lunch counter with a group of guys from the construction site?
You can have a place where no one, or no one of a certain privileged
group, will have his feelings hurt, or you can have a chance at a real
school or university, but you cannot have both at once.

Body and soul go together. I have been present at two faculty
meetings where women wept to get what they wanted. In one case,
a really friendly feminist was pushing for approval of a course to be
called "Gender and Genocide," on how male and female victims of
the Nazi Holocaust reacted to it in different ways. When a friend of
mine suggested some other title because that one sounded like a
jingle, she burst into tears—and that was the end of the discussion.
Women (think of a mother bear) will take attacks as aimed at their
persons, and as threatening destruction; they cannot afford not to.
The children (and the bearer of children) must be protected at all
costs. "The female of the species is more deadly than the male," said
Kipling, thinking of that motherly imperative. It's different with men.
My intellectual opponent is my wrestling partner, the enemy who is
my friend because he makes me stronger.

And so men will be the greatest intellectual fighters in our midst. If social media shows anything, it is this: men fight for ideas. I am not saying that women never do so; I can think of quite a few examples right away, including my stalwart and beloved wife and daughter. But when they do so, it is seldom with relish. Men are far more likely to wrestle with their own friends over definition, historical accuracy, logical or moral implication, and analogy, and far less likely to lose those friends when they do so. There is something in them that enjoys the opposition. If they are silenced—if our workplaces, our schools, and our public forums will not suffer men to take up arms against slackness, folly, and untruth—then we are a nation of weaklings. And no such nation is long for this world.

The *effete* are literally *effoeti*, meaning that they are all *out of offspring*. They are men with no potency in their loins, women with no fertility in their wombs. It is more a cultural than a physical condition, but it is a powerful instance of the body-soul union of man that an age so poor in cultural creation is also so poor in children. We commit a slow sexual suicide—to use George Gilder's prescient and incisive phrase—in both ways at once. Geld the men and spay the women, and you bid farewell to the future.

CHAPTER TWO

Agency

"If there is anything," says the mother, "which could reconcile me to living so far away in the woods, it is seeing my men-folk make a nice bit of land." For the land is not just given.

"Make land!" was the phrase that the French homesteaders around Lac Saint-Jean used to sum up all they did, all "the heart-breaking labor that transforms the incult woods, barren of sustenance, to smiling fields, ploughed and sown." If you find the Lac Saint-Jean on a map of Quebec, you may well sense that the task was not only difficult, but almost absurd. Why would anyone want to farm that harsh, inhospitable land two hundred kilometers north of the Saint Lawrence River, where the summers are warm but short and the winters so long and cold?

Because it can be done, and the soil is rich. And because it stands as a challenge. The conquest is all.

The scene is from *Maria Chapdelaine*, Louis Hemon's novel of the hardy Quebecois. It is what he witnessed, what he himself lived. Imagine the father of a family, his hired man, his three sons—the youngest of whom has only just come into his growth—and a big sluggish horse, "making land." There are no backhoes, no bulldozers, no diesel-powered harrows. You have only your arms and legs and back, the horse, and a few tools that give you a real but modest mechanical advantage: axes, picks, shovels, wedges, pulleys, chains, levers. Your first job is to clear the trees, and that means not just cutting them down but *pulling them out*:

> Between the scanty fields of their clearing and the darkly
> encircling woods lay a broad stretch which the ax had but
> half-heartedly attacked. A few living trees had been cut
> for timber, and the dead ones, sawn and split, fed the
> great stove for a whole winter; but the place was a rough
> tangle of stumps and interlacing roots, of fallen trees too
> far rotted to burn, of others dead but still erect amid the
> alder scrub.
>   Thither the five men made their way one morning and
> set to work at once, without a word, for every man's task
> had been settled beforehand.

The labor is grueling. The father and his eldest son swing their axes at either side of a tree, in rhythm, notching it above and below, until there is but a strip of trunk "by some miracle holding the tree erect." If the men fail to achieve that miracle, the badly managed cut will break the trunk too soon, bending the cut portion of the tree into a hump and leaving almost as much work again to saw it through, without gravity to assist. But the strip gives way, the trunk leans, and the two men step back and watch, "shouting at the same instant a warning of the danger."

The tree is down, but what now? It depended on how heavy the tree was. If it was not too heavy for the hired man and the eldest son at the utmost extent of their strength, they each took an end, "clasping their strong hands beneath the trunk, and then raised themselves—backs straining, arms cracking under the stress—and carried it to the nearest heap with short unsteady steps, getting over the fallen timber with stumbling effort." If it was too heavy even for that, then the youngest son came with the horse "dragging a tug-bar with a strong chain; this was passed around the trunk and fastened, the horse bent his back, and with the muscles of his hindquarters standing out, hauled away the tree which scraped along the stumps and crushed the young alders to the ground."

And this was the *easy* part of the work, because it involved only things above ground. The hard part was what to do with the stumps and the roots. The men had to dig around the stumps, one chopping away at the roots spreading level to the ground, while the other tries to work from underneath, or strains against a lever to raise the stump just a bit and sever some of the hundreds of bonds that anchor it down. The horse too must labor, once the stump is clear enough for a chain to be passed around it through a pulley, and that poor faithful friend of man strains with all his heart to yank the monstrous thing out of the earth.

The work takes three weeks, dawn to dusk—sweat, filth, frustration, doggedness, and final victory, so that the earth may be plowed up and seeds scattered, and the real work of farming begin.

The Arrow

The old alchemical symbol for mercury, both the element and the planet, was well chosen to denote also the masculine: the circle with an arrow pointing outward. There is something about masculine action and intelligence that has an *arrow* to it, and arrows pierce.

The wearisome objection arises: Boys, we hear, only *learn* such restless activity. They do not engage in it by nature. Our customs regarding sex could be wholly different. Let us consider just how absurd the objection is—how it defies not only everything that we know about the physiology and the behavior of mammals, but also the testimony of human cultures in every climate, in every age, and at every stage of technological development. Think of what it would mean if the expectations for boys and girls were really as unpredictable from culture to culture as, say, language is. *Dominus pastor meus*, says the pious man praying the psalm in Latin. *Adonai ro'i*, says the pious man two thousand miles away, praying in Hebrew. *Yr Arglwydd yw fy mugail*, says the Welshman. *The Lord is my shepherd*, says the Englishman. Go to a strange land, and you have not the slightest idea what anyone is saying, unless he accompanies his speech with the smiles or frowns or hand gestures that seem universal to mankind. But in that same strange land you will recognize immediately the behaviors of boys and girls, and men and women, that you are accustomed to in your own land; they will be as familiar to you as laughter is, though they will be manifest in a variety of ways in accord with the tasks to be done. You are an explorer going among the Eskimos, and you know immediately that the men, not the women, will be spearing the seals. You will see boys playing games on the ice, just as you might see boys playing games on the fields of Eton. *You are already proficient in that language*, because it is common to all mankind. Almost the reverse of what the feminist says is true: you can try your hardest to train the boy *not* to be a boy, and either you will fail miserably or you will make a masculine parody-doll out of him—Ken, with lipstick.

We know small boys are fascinated with machines. They do not want to cuddle the soldier-doll. They want to use it as a machine: a battering ram, a pile driver. In every boy there is something of the Coyote of happy memory, who constructs the wildest mechanical traps imaginable, often with blueprints scrawled over with vectors, to catch the scrawny little Road Runner. Is there an old abandoned building at the end of the road, barred shut? Break a window in back and crawl through, to explore. Is there a big tree hanging over the deep end of the lake? Climb it, nailing steps to its side. Shimmy far out along one of the stoutest limbs, parallel to the ground and thirty or forty feet above it. Fasten a thick rope to that limb, and you have hours and hours of joy. I am not saying that no girl *can* do such a thing. But, left to their own preferences, few girls *would* do it. If you see a rope swing like that, you will think immediately that boys have made it, and you will be right. Feminists themselves would think the same, though they might not like it.

The first but hardly the last aim of the restless masculine activity symbolized by the arrow is to change the face of the earth. When God curses Adam and Eve, the punishments are different. The woman will have pains in childbirth, and her relation to Adam will be troubled; she will desire him, and he will exercise domination over her. It is a fall from innocent desire and freely acknowledged hierarchy. The man, though, is cursed in his *labor*. The ground will bring forth thorns and thistles, and he will have to eat his bread in the sweat of his brow. "Idleness had been worse," says Milton's Adam, when he carefully considers the curse, seeing a blessing hidden in it. For man must work. The earth gives him the opportunity, even as it resists him, fights him. Whether man would have it any other way is another matter. It is the way it is.

The boy with his rope is the Roman engineer with his many ingenious tools for surveying, leveling, and measuring angles. Again we meet the arrow. You are living in Rome in the fourth century BC. Rome is a growing regional power, but it has nothing like the prestige that we now associate with it. Most of the Italian peninsula is not under Roman authority. And yet the city is already growing fast. It is full of people, and people need water. The Tiber River is nearby, but that is also where the sewage goes, and in any case the Romans are aware that the water in the river's mostly stagnant areas near the Tiber's mouth is not healthy. It breeds malaria (borne by mosquitoes, though the Romans didn't know that) and other diseases.

How do you get fresh water to a city that will soon be bursting with more than a million people? The arrow, the arrow. If nature does not come humbly with her gifts, compel her to comply: *change the face of the land.* When we think of Roman aqueducts, we should consider not just the engineering wonders the men accomplished, but the fact that they would conceive of such things at all.

There are springs eight miles away. You want their water. That is the challenge, which for the Romans was rather on the order of going to the moon for us—with the important difference that the Romans were after something that ordinary people must depend on for their health and their lives.

You need to build channels for the water, and you need to fashion pipes, too, because sometimes the water will have to go underground, *through* an intervening hill. If a river and its defile are in your way, you may need bridges, as at the famous Pont-du-Gard aqueduct bringing water into Nimes, France. Even if you do not have to build bridges, you will need stone, thousands and thousands of tons of it, for the piers to support the channels. You will need bricks or lead for the surface over which the water will flow. You need clay or lead for the pipes. You need to get the water to flow *gently* in the right direction: If your gradient is too steep, the aqueduct will be prone to overflow, and the water will be wasted. If it is not steep enough, the water will pool up, lose its sediment, stagnate, dam up, and spill.

The Romans used a gradient of one foot decline for every three hundred to seven hundred horizontal feet. Imagine a triangle five hundred feet long, one foot high, with a hypotenuse of five hundred feet and *one-eighth of an inch.* There's your triangle for the aqueduct.

Now do that for a course of five miles, and you have the *simplest* of the aqueducts leading into the city. Or rather you have the bare backbone of it, because you are going to need a spring-house to collect the water before it goes into the channel; you are going to have to cut down and uproot trees in the way of the course; you will need conduits to bring the water to public fountains and baths and private homes; you will need valves to start and stop the flow, or to regulate it to the proper extent. And besides the obviously necessary steady crews of overseers and repairmen, there must be a political network of responsible men along the course of the aqueduct, in case a sudden storm or heavy rain requires immediate and drastic action.

The sheer magnitude of the task boggles the mind. Where do you get the lead? Where do you get the clay and the stone? Where do you get the iron to make the tools that you need to procure the clay and cut the stone? Where do you get the wheels and the sledges to transport the materials? How do you build the winches to get large blocks off the ground to set them in the right place? You require, simultaneously, all the skills of mining, field-clearing, quarrying, metalworking, stone masonry, brickmaking, machine-construction—and *surveying*.

For it's one thing to say that you want the channels to drop only one foot for every five hundred feet. It's another thing to do it. The eye must be magnified in its power even more than the muscles must be. Tools, tools! Consider just one of them: the *chorobates*. Imagine a twenty-foot-long bench. How do you make it? With what kind of wood? How do you plane it? Plumb lines—so called because of the lead weights (Latin *plumbum*) at the ends of them—are attached to hang from both ends of the bench. The weights, pointed at the bottom, line up with notches cut in the bench at excruciatingly precise intervals. If the bench is level, the notches will be identical. You want them to be just a hair to one side of identical—in order to achieve your imperceptible-to-the-eye gradient of one foot of decline for every three hundred to seven hundred horizontal feet. But on windy days the plumb lines won't do you any good. So you have a groove cut into the top of the bench, where you can drop a little water and watch its flow, in the manner of a modern-day level.

I have not mentioned that the aqueduct must pass through land that might be owned by private citizens. Then you will need laws of eminent domain and fair recompense for public use. And if there are graveyards or other sacred places in the way, then you must skirt them, and *that* must be anticipated hundreds of feet in advance, because although your aqueduct can manage some gentle angles, you want to keep them to a minimum at all costs. The whole of it is a complex of games, mechanical, mathematical, and political.

Embarrassment, defeat, and futility meet you at every pass. If you are soft, you will not succeed. If you are soft, you will not attempt it in the first place. We know that when the soldiers were not on the frontier holding the line against barbarian invaders from the east and the north, the Roman army was essentially an army corps of engineers, building roads and dredging harbors and doing all sorts of other magnificent things. When you stop to consider it, the two forms of work are really one. The man who fights the barbarian who would storm his city and lay it waste is the man who fights the resistance and stubbornness of nature and makes the city in the first place. He is moved to conquer.

Multiply that project by innumerable thousands, just for the Roman Empire. Multiply those thousands by millions more, everywhere. When some women say, "We should wield power now, after men have made so bad a job of it," I wonder if they have bothered to consider what the job has been. I wonder if they even ask where their water comes from.

Making the City Possible

It is absurd to complain that men have not built cities exactly to one's liking, when without the stubborn daring of men—a daring that can be underappreciated precisely because it is so matter-of-fact—there would be no cities in the first place.

"Ordinarily," wrote one Charles Barnard at the beginning of a long essay called "The New Croton Aqueduct" (*The Century Magazine*, December 1889), "a dwelling-house, measuring say 33 by 35 feet, and standing where the rainfall is not less than 45 inches in a year, will collect on an average about 90 gallons of water per day; that is, supposing that all the water that falls in the area of the building is saved, that none is allowed to evaporate, and that the cistern is big enough to hold the excess of water in the wet months." That is the matter-of-fact language of a man with a job in mind, compressing it into numbers and applying them mercilessly. As he says, much water will be lost, and dry years will yield much less to begin with. People need water, and a five-story tenement in New York City, with the same roof surface as the single dwelling place, will provide daily for the five families and their twenty-five persons "only a trifle over three and a half gallons each," in which case New York City might as well shrink to the size of a small oasis in the Sahara.

Thus, when the population of the city reached 300,000, "it became necessary to obtain more water than could be supplied by the wells or roof tops," and so the men built the first Croton Aqueduct, diverting the water of the Croton River, thirty miles away, into the bustling city. It was completed in 1842. An endless supply, it seemed at the time—but New York City kept on growing, and, since people are profligate with what they do not themselves sweat for, the city faced some grave problems. People who lived on the lower floors of the tenements used all the water they wanted, leaving those on the upper floors with little. Pumps helped out for a while, and water tanks on the roofs, but that was not enough, and the city fathers decided that a new aqueduct, also running from the Croton River, would have to be built.

This would be a feat that, like the Roman aqueducts, was simultaneously a matter of engineering, calculation, foresight, and political action. Sentiment could not be permitted to intrude. The people who lived along the Croton, says Barnard, were "plain folks, quite as selfish, quite as indifferent to sanitary laws, and quite as firm in their belief in their right to do as seems to them fit, as the rest of us." Hence they used the river both as a source of power and as a sewer for their refuse. We should not judge them harshly, because we do the same in our time—except that our selfish indifference is more often moral than hydrological, and therefore it does more harm.

Barnard goes on to give the reader maps of the 338.82-square-mile watershed, reports of the inches of rainfall yearly recorded at Boyd's Corner (the reservoir at the head of the stream), and an account of the *billions of gallons* of water already stored in that reservoir and the Middle Branch reservoir, accurate to the million gallon. He tells us, with great care, of one difficulty after another surmounted by the doggedness and the ingenuity of man. For you cannot just say *Let us pipe water into the city from thirty miles away* and have done with it, as if it were just an affair of moving some object from one place to another. All kinds of problems must be foreseen and solved before they occur. When the Romans built their aqueducts far above ground, they had no need to worry whether the water would be clean, but this water would have to be brought into the city by underground pipes. What would happen if a pipe was damaged and filth got into the water? You can't just cut off the water in miles of pipe and search them to find the problem. You need access relatively close to every possible site of a problem. So you have to provide "a number of outlets or 'blow-offs' where the water can be drawn off from the whole or a part of the tunnel." This problem was made more acute by another, which was that the path of the aqueduct required two places where it had to sink considerably *and then rise again*. In the first, it had to go beneath a swamp; in the second, below the Harlem River. At these places the millions and millions of gallons had to be drawn up again by "inverted siphons."

We are treated to sketches and blueprints of gatehouses, blow-offs, waste weirs, shafts, tunnels, caves, and pipes, all requiring the work of men's hands and shoulders and legs and backs, magnified by clever water-powered or steam-powered machines, but without any of the great earth-moving equipment we take for granted today. "The maximum progress in any one week," says Barnard of the vertical shafts that had to be excavated, "was twenty one feet," hardly the height of a two-story house. "In this enormous labor at one time," he says, "ten thousand men were employed, with hundreds of mules and horses and a great number of steam engines, and their labors underground were lighted by scores of electric lights." How do you get the materials to them—including food? On barges and canal boats sent up the East River to the Harlem docks, to the New York and Northern railroad line, and that would include the 163,000,000 bricks to form the arches and supports for the tunnel. And what happens if the rock through which the tunnel must go is soft? That is not a boon. It is a problem. Then the tunnel must be shored up by "timbering," just as men do for the walls of a mine. Fortunately, Barnard says, it was not usually necessary; only 39,000 feet of the tunnel required it—*only* seven and a half miles. I wonder how many people understand that the work of men has often bordered upon madness.

Barnard does not tell us whether any men died in the making of this wonder, or whether anyone lost a limb in an explosion or to the recalcitrance of a machine. But he does give us a firsthand account of what some of the work was like. He went down into the depths himself to see it. His entry, at a place under repairs and by a ladder wet with clay, "was rather depressing." As he and his guides went on, "the spot of sunlight behind us faded away to only a yellow star that at last went out." Sometimes by the light of their lamps they caught a glow, a strange white mark on the walls, "where the engineers or the inspectors had measured the work or left traces for future measurements or inspections." Mostly they heard only the rushing of the stream at their feet, but "then might come a distant sound, or rather reverberation, like the ghost of a thunder peal," and they could not be sure from which direction the sound came. "The lines of brick stretch on and on," he says, "in uniform, unbroken precision." It must be so, if the water is going to flow right. "The sloping floor never changes its exact angle, the walls are ever exactly in line, and high above the head is the arched roof. It is the perfection of mechanical work stretching ever onward through darkness."

I find one sketch in Barnard's essay especially suggestive. Its caption is "Working on the Pipe Line." A man in a hard hat, evidently the overseer, stands in profile. His is the only face you see. Another man, with tools strapped to his suspenders, stands on a platform, his back to us, where a large section of pipe is attached to a block and tackle suspended from a triangular wooden frame. The other men, hunched over, one leg planted in back and the other thrust forward, lean all their weight and their strength against pry-bars to roll another section of pipe and lift it into place. We can hardly understand such work now, and not just because it is gruelingly physical. It demands a constant self-denial, a self-effacement. It says to the men what the battle says to a soldier: "You are not the central thing. This work is. Do it."

The Croton Aqueduct was one project—a big project for sure, but only one. Again, multiply by thousands and thousands, everywhere.

The World Does Not Run on Magic

At a recent hearing before the Senate Committee on Homeland Security, the CEO of Colonial Pipeline made an admission which illustrates quite well our negligence and improvidence. The company paid out nearly five million dollars in blackmail money to an unknown hacker, when the pipeline was shut down for several days. That, of course, was bad enough, and most of the man's testimony had to do with the technicalities of which government agency was notified and when and what the company's computer experts did to remedy the situation. But there was another piece of his testimony, one that you had to look hard to find in the news reports. He testified that most of the men who could operate the controls on the pipeline have died or retired, so that the 5,500-mile line must rely almost wholly upon computerized systems for its operation. That means, of course, that we are vulnerable to attacks by people who do not have to take a guard at gunpoint or dig a big hole somewhere that no one will notice.

Practical necessity required the engineers and the men who constructed the Croton Aqueduct to ensure that the system had *many* points of effective control, not one, lest some random accident in one place leave a million people without drinking water. But our technology has progressed to the point where, for a time, we can get away with running things on the cheap—and the irresponsible. This fact merits some consideration.

"Intersectionality" is the academic fad of our time asserting that various forms of prejudice against members of different groups inevitably intersect when someone belongs to more than one of the groups. The various "structures" of disadvantage overlap and intersect to the harm of certain designated minorities, including women, in whose case "minority" is a metaphorical term. It is a deterministic theory that reduces the immensely complex tangle and muddle of human relations to a formula, and it ignores the fact that human ingenuity is like intelligent water: If you try to dam it up here, it will spill out over there. If it is narrowed in scope, it will gain in force. The human mind is restless, and the human will is stubborn, and people will make a virtue of necessity.

The term "intersectionality" was coined by Kimberlé Williams Crenshaw, a black lawyer and professor of law at UCLA. Crenshaw is a feminist, and though she maintains that black men are not better off than black women, she pursues policies that, for the working-class family, are like prescribing blood thinner to someone who is hemorrhaging. Those families are in desperate need of strong, well-remunerated men who can support them—with what are and what practically must remain masculine skills and regions of activity. And yet Crenshaw has fought against any particular focus upon the needs of boys, and she has championed the Equality Act, which, with its promotion of women and gay men, is a dagger aimed at the heart of the healthy masculine camaraderie that builds aqueducts and lays pipelines.

The Colonial Pipeline was invented, created, and maintained by men with the technical skill to do so. Whatever we say about its invention and creation—though all of human history testifies to the boundlessly creative power of mechanically-minded men—certainly the *maintenance* had to be that way. Women were not going to do it then. And with an occasional outlier here or there, women are not going to do it now. If you call a plumber to deal with a sewer pipe that has backed up into your basement, it is a practical certainty that it is going to be a man, because the sheer strength required to deal with the valve rusted shut or with a section of pipe that has to be cut or muscled into place is like a threshold. If you cannot reach the threshold (and if you are a teenage boy or an old man, you are likely to fail), you cannot do that job. You cannot, as our women soldiers apparently do, ask the man next to you to give you a hand. All kinds of tasks involve such thresholds.

All right, then. Now suppose that you do not want to raise boys to be those men. How can you ensure that you fail at this basic task? First, you deny millions of boys a married father in the home; you pursue policies perversely designed to reward family breakdown. I am speaking of the preponderant case: boys are not going to learn how to wield a sledgehammer from their mothers. Second, you push college credentials, hugely expensive and of now dubious value as far as actual learning is concerned, so that most people who do not go to college must languish in low-paying and menial work. Instead of building the Brooklyn Bridge, they are wheeling carts of groceries at Walmart. Third, you divert resources away from high school boys who want to pursue the skilled trades. That has been a dreadful mistake.

If you go to the Museum of Industry in Stellarton, Nova Scotia, you can see relics of what used to be—within living memory—a program of education in the trades, on wheels, that went from place to place throughout the province. Boys took great advantage of it. It no longer exists, even though we still need technicians. Perhaps the people who run our schools have so little experience themselves, so little memory of physical labor in their shoulders and their hands, that it never occurs to them that the world cannot run on courses in sociology or on politically enlightened novels. They do not think, *Who is going to dig that well?* They trade not in fresh water, petroleum, electricity, uranium, titanium, and gold, but in words, and not well-chosen and historically grounded words at that. Margaret Atwood is at leisure to write about her Republic of Gilead, a dystopia in which women must submit their sexuality to their male masters, only because men carved *Canada* from the wild for her to write it in.

How, at this juncture, can we redirect resources to those high school boys? That is hard to figure, because we have committed ourselves to "equality," which in this case means that young men who do have the strength for skilled manual labor and the tolerance for risk and filth will be forced to be as useless as young women when it comes to maintaining something like the Colonial Pipeline. This "equality" comes at the expense of the common good. It is frankly absurd that we must rely upon a computer program—all things concentrated upon a single vulnerable point—and not upon a network of skilled men to maintain a pipeline that delivers 100 million gallons of gasoline, heating oil, and airplane fuel to Americans in the east *every day*.

Every lack presents an opportunity, but only if you have people with the inclination and the power to take it. Imagine what a Booker T. Washington would have made of this state of affairs. He would have hired pipeline technicians in a heartbeat and set them to training his young men to do the much-needed work. They would have made themselves indispensable, and when you are indispensable it does not matter what people think of you. They need you, they pay you. And in any case, do good work, and they will change their minds about you, even if they were ill-disposed in the beginning. Americans are now so tremendously incompetent that any generation of reasonably provident men, maneuvering themselves into work that only men such as they are can do, will enrich themselves in a generation and seize the levers of power in the next.

For what I am saying about this pipeline is true generally in the United States. Our infrastructure is a mess. Drive along our major highways, and what do you see? Roads designed for much lighter traffic than they now bear, substandard entrances and exits, ponderously slow repairs, bad lighting, general ugliness, vandalism when you approach the big cities. The junction between Interstates 93 and

95 in Massachusetts, in the densely populated Boston metropolitan area, is notoriously bad, and has been so for at least thirty years. Imagine what happens every day when four lanes of traffic must be narrowed down to two, around a long bend. Why has this bottleneck not been remedied long since? Well, who would do that work? And where has the money gone that might have hired the men to do it? Ride on a train into Philadelphia or New York, and note every site at which skilled labor might be employed to develop, to repair, to beautify, or to clean, and consider how many thousands—millions—of young men might find such work *if we were only raising young men capable of and willing to do it.*

Making that a national priority would go a long way toward solving several problems at once. We would replace vulnerable nerve centers with a practically invulnerable net. We would gain the benefits of safety, cleanliness, efficiency, and beauty. We would raise the hopes, the incomes, and the aims of the working class. We would make it suddenly possible for working-class men to marry young and with confidence. We would strengthen their families and take a small but important step toward reversing America's decline into single parenthood, with its results of loneliness, incapacity, and—for many a frustrated young man—crime. And those among us most likely to profit directly from it would be precisely the disadvantaged populations that those who preach about intersectionality say they want to help: think of African Americans.

So why don't we do these things?

Let me answer that question with another question: Who benefits most from the entry into the workplace of many millions of women of child-bearing age? The rich. They can afford the best day care. If they own businesses, they get the benefit of depressed labor costs, as more applicants chase the same jobs. It would be against their interest for one good income per household to become the rule again, rather than the exception. They get to enjoy two prime salaries for a single household, and they spend most of the overage in isolating themselves as far as possible from the working- and lower-middle class. It is against their bent toward self-isolation to be rubbing elbows with well-remunerated plumbers, carpenters, masons, miners, earth-movers, and welders, with their rough hands and sometimes rough ways. The feminism that denies the strength of young men—or damns it as "toxic masculinity"—and discourages the virtues that build family life intersects with the old-fashioned social and economic structures that keep the poor in their place.

There is still another reason why we do not form those working men: because we believe the world can run by magic. We believe in good magic and in bad magic. The bad magic is easy to see. We are awash in words, and that means we are awash in cant. We use labels to manage what might be a devilishly difficult thing to study—let us say, the relations between men and women. Instead of facing the great, mysterious, and many-featured universe of customs and laws adapted to different people's climate, agricultural opportunity, technological development, and religious faith, not to mention the innumerable physical distinctions between the sexes, we explain it all away with one word: "sexism." We then take the word for an existent thing, like bauxite, except that bauxite can be identified precisely and analyzed, whereas "sexism" is simply a form into which we press everything we see. It is not that men have always been impelled to work both by their nature and by the need to support women and free them up to care for children and maintain households, especially before modern technology rendered cooking, cleaning, and laundry a less than full-time job. "Sexism" kept women from having careers. It is not that men, at the highest grade, are better chess players than women. "Sexism" somehow causes all the chess champions to be men. *Why* it would bother to do so pointless a thing, and by what precise mechanism, no one explains. Indeed, if you ask for an explanation, you will be condemned as a tool of the sexist system. This is not to play with conic sections. It is just to argue in a circle—a magic circle.

We also believe in good magic. It seems that we assume the world can run in a magical way. We need only wish a thing, and it will happen, because *somebody* will take care of it, or rather *something*, a mysterious agent in a black box. To save the world from climate change, we should use electricity instead of burning fossil fuels. But where do we get the electricity? It must simply happen, like lightning from the sky. I dare say we have all read hundreds of articles on the need to provide power in a clean, efficient, and sustainable way. But how many address the fundamental problem posed: that is, that all electricity is generated by the brute physical fact of making a great shaft of magnetic metal turn? And once you face that fact, you confront other facts having to do with the quantity of force available, its reliability, the metals and plastics you must use to house the enormous and by no means simple turbine, the type of conductive wire wherein the electricity will be produced, the amount of the electricity, the pressure it exerts, the resistance it meets to its flow, the distance it must traverse, and more. You face the same kinds of problems as beset the builders of the Croton Aqueduct. What happens when the flow is interrupted at one point? Will everyone downstream from the interruption necessarily be without power? Are there "valves," so to speak, to control the flow? Are there conduits to siphon away any excess?

The ten thousand men who worked on the Croton Aqueduct at any one time had a broad array of practical and scientific skills. Where did they get them? Not mostly from school—only the few chief engineers would have gone (might have gone) to school to learn about hydraulics and geology. The vast majority of the men learned by work.

Women did not teach them that work, because—to mention another brute fact—women did not do that work, and could not do it, any more than prepubescent boys could do it. But because *no one* can do such work now, we must hand our safety and our welfare over to a computer program—at precisely a time when, more than ever, it would require the well-directed strength of young men to make our cities healthy once more and to raise strong families of responsible citizens.

Many a boy languishes in school because he finds no arrow there. Things are staid, routine. Perhaps there are arrows to pick up now and again, if you are the sort of boy who will look for them and not be too discouraged, and if the arrows available are fit for the kind of shooting you want to do. But the failure of boys in school—not this boy or that boy, but boys by the millions, despite the fact, attested by empirical investigation and the evidence of history, that they are at least the equals of their sisters in intelligence—suggests that the schools are quite simply bad for them. They stunt their growth. Intellectually and practically, the boys are like pale and spindly plants that have been kept indoors all the days of their lives.

And yet, obviously, we need these boys; it is criminally negligent to deny it. Consider how many young black men, in particular, are languishing, because their schools are—at their best—no great shakes, and because they lack the fathers in the home who would train them up in skill and strength. Everywhere you turn your eye in the United States, you will find ugliness, disrepair, vandalism, buildings left to rot—and unemployed or underemployed young men, disheartened, not worth marrying, and ready to cause trouble, since they can cause so little else.

Hope, the Spring of Action

We men rightly look with wonder upon a woman about to give birth and think, *How can she see beyond the suffering of the body, and the great pain she must undergo, to the child to come?* And women once looked with wonder on good and strong men, who grow better and stronger by obstacles and who seek out the fight for the sheer joy of it.

But you do not shoot the arrow without an aim, and you do not have an aim unless you believe you can hit the mark—and that the mark is worth hitting. It seems to me that boys in our schools have been given only targets that mean nothing to them, that are to aims that would rouse their masculine hearts as holding hands is to arm wrestling.

So I turn to a poem, from *The Century Magazine* (November 1889), by John Vance Cheney (1848–1922), a man such as we no longer make in America: he practiced law, he taught music, he was a postal clerk, he wrote essays and poems, and he became a librarian, overseeing the creation of branch libraries in San Francisco, till he finally was chosen to head the Newberry Library in Chicago. The poem's title is a verse from the prophet Jeremiah: "Is there any word from the Lord?" (37:17). The answer is yes, there is—but only the brave will hear it.

The first two stanzas come from the point of view of "the babblers" and "the craven," who say that "trust is outworn," that "naught can be done," that "the strong hand shakes, the warriors wail." Then comes the third stanza, and the voice of an American man in full confidence:

> Are we, forsooth, so helpless, we
> That vanquish air, and earth, and sea?
> The sun shines yonder; somewhere glows
> The old first hope, bright as a rose,
> The hope whose accent high
> Shall brand this whining lie.

That is not someone given to wringing his hands in helplessness or, worse, bemoaning the sins of his fathers, unwilling to acknowledge their achievements and too timid to take up the pious civilization-building task which they began. "Israel still has his God," he cries.

Men who are bold will not admit defeat. They did not do so in the time of David, when that young man and his outcast followers defeated the armies of King Saul. They did not do so when the Athenians crowded the Persians in the straits of Salamis and left their fleet a wreckage on the water:

> The seers, the prophets, poets—they
> See yet the good gold in the day;
> They of his line that conquered Saul
> Can crowd small cowards to the wall,
> They that were Athens' might
> Can put pale wraiths to flight.

Ah, poetry, the manly art of it, which has sunk in our time to picking at the scabs of a wounded self, or to the show but not the courage of moral offense—what might it do, if men began again to sing indeed?

> Poets, still red at heart, arise,
> Sing back the blue into the skies,
> Sing back the green into the grass,
> And bid these skulking phantoms pass:
> You, dauntless sons of song,
> Can blast this dastard wrong.

"Dauntless sons of song"? Where are they? We have smothered them in the crib or muffled them up in timidity, slovenliness, and indifference. But the heart of the man, the real thing, has not changed and will not change.

Let all who "know" better be content to whine in their prisons. Likewise for all who whisper into men's ears, serpent-like, that there is nothing for them to do, that love is a cheat, that there is no God above, that there is no song to sing:

> Once more, blest messengers, declare
> That love still lives, that life is fair;
> Say knowledge knows not, trust is all,
> And crush these wise which writhe and crawl!
> Wake, wake, your strains of fire,
> God's for us—strike the lyre.

I mean here to reject every philosophy that would cut the sinews of man. I once heard a young man who lived on the shores of Hudson Bay complain that for a native like him, a son of the aboriginal First Nations, there was nothing to look forward to in life except to become a hockey player or a chief. By "chief," he meant the head of a tribe, who gathers the money that the Canadian government gives bounteously to the tribe and then disburses it as he sees fit. The arrangement is not one to guarantee responsibility.

That young man was schooled in despair. All determinism is born either of despair or of the desire—on the part of those who are rich and powerful—to stay that way and to keep their supposed inferiors where they are. But men—who, being bigger and not made to bear children and take intimate care of the very young, are less bound to the exigencies of the body than women are—should never be told that there is nothing for them to do, that they are bound by some iron determining principle, whether neurological or social or political. Then they die inside, or their considerable energy and desire to take the world by the throat turns sour. Let them build things up, or they will burn things down.

And there is much for them to build. Every failure in one regard is an opportunity in another, and determinism be damned. There is no end of examples. Men have built schools. Not only did they quarry the stone and hew the timber to make the building rise. They quarried the mind and hewed the arts. They went on the attack. That frail fellow in the cubbyhole who cannot swing the sledgehammer is on the attack: he has set himself a seemingly insurmountable problem. Everyone knows that the sum of two squares may itself be a square: as $9 + 16 = 25$. But can the sum of two non-zero cubes itself be a cube? Or the sum of two integers raised to any single power—can it be an integer raised to that power?

That is Fermat's Last Theorem, the object of intense mathematical study for more than 300 years after Pierre de Fermat said in 1637 that he had developed a proof that no such solutions exist for any power greater than 2. You may ask, "What difference does it make whether it is so or not?" If you look about you, you will see yourself surrounded by objects whose conception, structure, and function depend upon higher mathematics: take, for example, the gentle curve of an airplane's wings that allows it to fly rather than to plummet like a stone or bump along the ground till it crashes into a hill. When Fermat made his conjecture, no such things existed, nor were they anything but the idle doodles of mathematical daydreamers, such as Leonardo da Vinci.

Why do they doodle and dream—and beat their heads against such abstract problems? That is like asking the man why he wants to climb the mountain or sail the sea. It is there. He wants to map the tunnels of the cave. He wants to articulate the skeleton of the creature washed up on the beach. He wants to see what will happen to sand if it is fired by lightning. "Wha' makes it goo?" asked the three-year-old boy James

Clerk Maxwell, following along beside his father as he inspected the machines on his estate in Scotland. For men, the "go" of something with immediate profit is not ultimately different from the "go" of abstractions, of the creations or the discoveries of his mind. What makes those numbers go?

A ten-year-old boy named Andrew Wiles heard about Fermat's conjecture and was amazed that something so easy to express had evaded proof or disproof for so long. He said to himself that *he was going to prove it one way or the other*, and he went straight to the library to pick up a book about it. He had the soul of a pioneer, an explorer. He did not say the things that would have ruled the quest out from the beginning: that it was of no use, that it meant nothing, that it could not be done. Kurt Goedel had proven that in any system at least as complex as arithmetic, there will be statements that are well defined and true but not demonstrably so. But if you think at the outset that *this particular proof* cannot be done, you will not try.

Wiles became a mathematician—one of the greatest in the world. When he was thirty-three years old, a suggestion from an apparently unrelated field of mathematics set him to working at the theorem again, for six years, in secret. His proof, published in 1993, shook the mathematical world, and when an error was found in one of the steps, he spent another year and a half searching for a way to correct the error, and he succeeded in the end. Seven and a half years of work, then, most of it without any cooperation from friends or mentors or students, resulting in one long mathematical paper—but gold, pure gold, or whatever substance would be to gold as gold is to rust.

Why do men do things like that? Well, imagine what kind of creature would engage in such behavior: a creature powerfully moved to attack, to conquer; undeterred by discouragement; capable of setting personal feelings to the side; capable indeed of an ascetic existence, like that of a hermit in the desert or a man of the mountains.

There are not many people on earth who can understand Wiles's theorem, but every man, I believe, can understand his motive force, the arrow.

Go to a different field. Take linguistics. You are Jacob Grimm, of the Brothers Grimm. You have been set aflame by the study of Germanic antiquities. That includes the folktales that every child is acquainted with, such as the tale of Aschenputtel—Cinderella. But you cannot stop there. You have read the great romances of the German Minnesaenger—the *Parsifal* of Wolfram von Eschenbach, for example. You want to do for the German language something like what the French encyclopedists have done: you want to bring together in one comprehensive vision all of German vocabulary and grammar. But that will require you to investigate all the dialects you can, present and past. And that leads you in turn to other Germanic languages, to Dutch, to English, to the languages of Scandinavia. Nor can you stop there; your research leads you to ancient forms of those languages, and even to languages that no longer exist, such as Gothic, a Germanic tongue from the east preserved only in large fragments of a translation of the New Testament prepared by the Arian bishop and missionary Ulfilas in the fourth century.

Restless, relentless, Grimm saw that he could not fully understand the import of the ancient words without a knowledge of other ancient tongues that were not Germanic but were in the same large family of tongues we now call Indo-European—Latin and Greek, but also Sanskrit, the holy language of the Hindus of India, and many others. What Grimm did revolutionized the study of languages. He became the first man to posit a general law of sound changes: Grimm's Law, which showed why a root that gives us *pater* and *piscis* and *pes* in Latin gives us *father* and *fish* and *foot* in English, or why a root that gives us *thygater* and *thymos* and *thoris* in Greek gives us *daughter* and *dust* and *door* in English. Grimm's Law is a complex one, regarding a kind of great wheel of consonants of various kinds shifting position with stunning regularity, whose apparent exceptions reveal still other laws in play. It was the first such law ever discovered, and it is no exaggeration to say that everyone who deals with the transformation of the sounds of words in any language whatsoever is building upon the foundation that Grimm established.

Why did he do it? It was of no immediate profit to him. It made him no friends; it brought him no power. To do it, he had to make his slow way into an untracked wilderness of hundreds of thousands of words, of a place-name here and a proper name there, words whose existence could only be known from, say, a stray reference in a text from the ancient world—and again with no social encouragement. Other than understanding, other than knowledge, what does Grimm's Law give us? But knowledge itself is precious.

I will give another example. I have often written that wherever you find numbers, you will find men and boys, and wherever you find men and boys, you will find numbers. I am not speaking of mathematicians here, but of a masculine drive to get to the heart of a thing by means of the mathematical arrow. You are Bill James, who ate and drank and played and slept baseball from his earliest years. He attacked an apparently impossible-to-solve problem: "How can we evaluate the players of one age as against players of another age, when their statistical records are so obviously different?" If Carl Yastrzemski leads the league in batting in 1968, at .301, is that like Rogers Hornsby leading his league in batting in 1924, at .424? Or what exactly is a home run worth to the team when the average number of runs per team per game is 4.0, as opposed to when it is 3.8? Or exactly what, if anything, does the typical team gain by attempting to steal a base, or by attempting to bunt a runner from first to second? Or what is a team's record likely to be, if they have scored X runs and have given up Y?

When James was asking these questions, they were of no consequence to anyone but himself and a few baseball fanatics like him.
No team had hired him as an analyst. He would eventually make a
career of it, but at the time it was not at all obvious that such a career
would ever exist. What he began is now called "sabermetrics," a word
coined from the name of the Society for American Baseball Research,
which he helped to found. If you now go to the internet's best site for
baseball statistics, you will see quite literally hundreds of statistical
categories, each based in turn upon millions of numbers, evaluated
according to formulas that James and his few fellows developed in
their basic form and then adjusted to square better with reality; it is
a whole world of summation, evaluation, comparison, and compre-
hension. Once again, the obvious question is, "Why would anyone
do that?"

Men like James are driven by what psychologist Ellen Winner
has called the "rage to master," a consuming and obsessive interest
in what fascinates them, often to the exclusion of more ordinary
pursuits, so that they tend to be lonely as children and to have few
friends even as adults; they do not fit into any routine, instead they
make their own rules about how to learn and even how the object
they pursue is to be conceived. It is hard to imagine how the human
race could have survived if women had been as *antisocial* and
unfriendly and *unpleasant* as men can be, and as the most creative
men often are. I do not mean to suggest something strictly negative
by those adjectives. Thomas Edison had nothing *against* society. It is
simply that he was strangely indifferent to it. It got in his way. Even
his family got in his way. He would sleep on a table in his laboratory
and engage in work, which to him was an obsessive form of play,
seventeen or eighteen hours a day. The basketball player Jerry Lucas
was not opposed to making friends. It is simply that he had more
important things to do, and he did them in an utterly unique way.

He kept a running total in his mind of all the statistics logged by every player in every game he played, and so obsessive was this rage, this need to have things exactly as they should be, that if the score-keeper made an error, or if it was not clear to which player the scorer had awarded an assist, Lucas would approach him when time was out to make sure what was what. That did not endear him to his fellow players, but Lucas did not care. *He memorized what every player did*, and that was how he gained an advantage over them; and this was long before our age of computer analytics. Indeed, Lucas could memorize large sections of the Manhattan telephone book, and later in life he memorized the New Testament and became a Christian.

Or consider the sheer uselessness of the chess prodigy. In 1924, Alexander Alekhine, one of the greatest players who ever lived, played twenty-six games simultaneously, against strong competition, *while blindfolded*—winning sixteen, losing five, and drawing five. No human being can be all things to all people at all times. There is a cost to such accomplishment, or rather an immediately and intrinsically exacted cost to the personality and the mind driven to such accomplishment. Mozart's father once said of the boy that he could not see. It was not that he was blind, but that he simply *did not see* the things around him, did not notice them, because they were not part of his fascination.

The rage is inward. If you are very fortunate, people around you will encourage it or give it some scope. Certainly it is almost never encouraged by school; the boy genius succeeds usually *in spite of school*, or because his father had him taught privately, so that he could pursue the sole love without distraction. Thus did Mozart's father, and Pascal's father, and the chess prodigy Paul Morphy's father. But the rage is simultaneously satisfying to the boy or the man and unpleasant to others, sometimes even to himself. If you are going to do something that shakes up the field of action, says Winner, you will have to accept being hated and denounced by others, but you cannot care for that—you do not aim to please everyone; you aim to please yourself by mastering the domain.

Shakespeare was the greatest man of letters who ever lived, but he was the object of bitter contempt by the older playwright Robert Greene, who called him an "upstart crow," "the only shake-scene in a country." Dante earned the contempt of his contemporary Bonagiunta of Lucca for introducing the theological and philosophical terms and ideas of the schools into love poetry, and Dante appears to have been stung by the criticism, but that did not deter him; in fact, there is a deliberate standoffishness or challenging posture to his great early work, *La Vita nuova*, that appears to say, "Interpret me if you dare." We might say that Dante was a born outcast, long before his enemies in Florence condemned him to leave the city on pain of death and confiscated his goods.

John Milton cared for neither bishop nor king, and he wrote his masterpiece *Paradise Lost* after he had gone blind. His enemies called his blindness a judgment of God against him for having been an apologist for the arrest, trial, and execution of King Charles I of England. Milton was thrown in prison, and it required the assistance of his fellow poet and both-sides-playing statesman Andrew Marvell to have him released. But Milton did not care to please the masses. So he writes at the beginning of Book VII of *Paradise Lost*, in his invocation to Urania (announcing that most of the rest of the poem will take place on earth):

Half yet remains unsung, but narrower bound
Within the visible diurnal sphere;
Standing on earth, nor rapt above the pole,
More safe I sing with mortal voice, unchanged
To hoarse or mute, though fallen on evil days,

On evil days though fallen, and evil tongues;
In darkness, and with dangers compassed round,
And solitude; yet not alone, while thou
Visit'st my slumbers nightly, or when morn
Purples the east; still govern thou my song,
Urania, and fit audience find, though few. (7.21–31)

That is the talk of a man who cannot let anything stand in his path. He made his daughters write down what he composed, sometimes dreaming the lines in his early morning sleep. We do not know whether they enjoyed doing so. We can suspect that it never occurred to Milton to ask them.

The masculine personality, which aims at creation, accepts rejection and opposition—can even thrive on them. A man will stand naked in the arena, knowing that the wild animals are just beyond gates that his enemies are ready to open. In *A Room of One's Own*, Virginia Woolf asks us to imagine a Judith Shakespeare endowed with the same genius as her brother, but without the same opportunity to express it because she did not enjoy the quiet that he must have enjoyed. Whether Shakespeare ever enjoyed quiet I do not know; the lives of geniuses are often tumultuous. These men can make the artificial quiet they need by blocking out many of the pleasures that other people enjoy—and that is but the masculine personality writ large. (Autism—a condition that is disproportionately male, to an overwhelming degree—essentially means carrying a room of your own around with you, into the heat of battle.)

Think of the painter Caravaggio. He lost his father when he was six and his mother when he was thirteen. He had a violent temper and was never far away from a brawl—one of which ended in his killing another young man. He was both celebrated and abominated. He may have died of poison. But he was revolutionary in his work: he would not idealize his sacred subjects, but often showed them for the peasants and the sinners they were. He had an immense influence on Rembrandt, who, though not a violent man, would, like Caravaggio, experience rejection and poverty—and be unwilling to change one whit to please the public.

In "The Appearance of the Child Prodigy 10,000 Years Ago: An Evolutionary and Developmental Explanation" (2009), the neurophysiologist Larry R. Vandervert discusses the links between early visuospatial processing in the infant, "heightened emotional-attentional control," and superior working memory—all of which characterize such children. The cerebellum, which controls working memory, is the part of the brain where for-motor activity—for action—is centered. Now suppose that in boys and men the work of the mind is akin to the kind of action that the male sex enjoys: making things happen, wrenching, twisting, pounding, cutting, building, tracking down, and killing. Doesn't that shed light on their habits of intellectual struggle and conquest?

Vandervert discusses the case of a boy called "Geoffrey," who at age five had not written a single word, but thirteen months later had written 1,600 pages of increasingly sophisticated text. What piques my interest here is the markedly masculine cast of the boy's mind. He demanded that his parents draw for him realistic pictures of Montreal, where they lived—with all the angles and the perspective right. When he was four, he spent eight months building up in his bedroom, with toys, stuffed animals, and cardboard boxes, a model of Montreal as he saw it in his mind's eye. He would gaze on it for hours, talking to himself and rearranging things to make the model a better fit for what he had in his mind. He was reasoning visually, abstracting from objects their meaning for the model, while separating out, placing in the compartment of not relevant, what might appeal to a normal child. Indeed, his visual reasoning flowered and became linguistic reasoning when he began to write, and this, too, was self-directed. He was thinking about his thoughts.[1]

We might do well to wonder whether a masculine cast of mind is oriented not simply to the spatial and visual as such—because in fact many boys and men are not terribly interested in machines—but in all things as treated with a kind of spatial and visual schema, including language. Imagine a small boy who asks his parents for a Christmas present: a full street map of the city where they live, so that he can commit the names and the directions to memory. That was me. Or a four-year-old who memorizes the books of the Bible in order and writes the first letter of their names in a long acronym, over and over—along with the entries in the daily TV guide; that was me. Or the shapes and the positions of all fifty states, their rivers, and their cities, so as to draw them freehand. That was me. I still do things like that. It is hard to explain why, but the "rage to master" gets hold of my soul, so that I relax by working, by performing feats of memory and manipulation as I lie in bed before falling asleep. My professor of Middle English in graduate school grew up next to a farmer who recited the whole of *Paradise Lost* to himself as he was plowing the fields. I want to be able to do the same, and I will someday, though I do not have a plow.

Put it this way. When boys play with dolls they turn them into objects to be manipulated rather than treating them as persons to be cared for, and when they play with language itself they may do the same kinds of things. That would explain why those forms of literature that are clearly and hierarchically articulated—in the way that mathematical formulas and maps and complex machines are—are overwhelmingly masculine: epic poetry and poetic drama, for example. Women have been writing a lot of poetry in English for the last two hundred years, and still the two greatest female poets in history, Sappho and Emily Dickinson, excelled in the short, concentrated, passionate lyric, not in the vast and sweeping epic.

We can say the same about concepts. Suppose you asked Thomas Aquinas what he felt about whether you can prove necessarily that God exists. He might say that the question had excited him since he was a boy. But that is not exactly what you mean. His excitement is intellectual, and it has little to do with how he feels about himself or about other people. The boy Blaise Pascal, said his sister, played with conic sections the way other children played with toys, and I have no doubt that he did, and that she meant more than that he was always preoccupied with them. They fascinated him. They were his invisible friends, bathed in the light and the colors of the mind. They were his toys. If you asked Thomas whether the proof that God necessarily exists energized him, whether it spurred him on, whether it stood like a challenger in the field, swaggering and daring him to, I am sure he would reply that it did. But if you asked whether his emotions determined his response to the question, he would answer that his feelings were not pertinent.

It doesn't matter what I feel, I imagine Thomas saying. *The truth does not care about my feelings*. Then he would return with quiet and intense satisfaction to the next question to be attacked, the next patch of intellectual ground to be mastered.

Take that hill, men.

CHAPTER THREE

The Team

All my life I have heard feminists complain about male groups in politics, education, the sciences, and business, calling them by the scornful name "the old boys' clubs." The assumption is that the character of such groups is either stupid or malignant, and that they are designed to keep women out. The feminists never ask a couple of obvious questions: Why have men in every society formed such groups in the first place? How are such groups different from other forms of social gathering? What do such groups achieve, and to what degree is the all-male character of the group central to their achievement of those things? Unwittingly the feminists themselves suggest that these groups are as *natural* to men as they are to boys, who cannot be accused of wielding any economic or political power.

When it comes to all-male groups, contrasting men with boys is misleading—as is attempting to draw a distinction between nature and "social constructs." As Aristotle observed, man is by nature a social animal. No one says of such social mammals as wolves and dogs that they wouldn't behave the way they do if they hadn't been taught to behave that way, or that they might behave far differently if their elders taught them otherwise. Of course they are taught how to behave—because the inner promptings of their nature demand it. There is no contrasting a natural wolf pack over here with a socially constructed wolf pack over there. The wolf pack is at once fully natural and fully social.

With man, who has free will and whose intellect opens for him a boundless field of action, it may appear to be otherwise—it may seem that we can cut loose from human nature itself and have any kind of society we like. But that is a delusion, as the brutal experiments against human nature in the last hundred years have shown. Must we continue to suffer one Soviet Union after another, just because we think ourselves too high and mighty to learn from our own nature and the distilled experiences of billions of people preserved in our traditions?

The verses that describe the creation of man in Genesis are wiser here than a hundred books of sociology. For in one sense man is set apart from all the rest of creation. "Let us make man in our image, after our likeness," says God, "and let them have dominion over the fish of the sea, and over the birds of the air, and over the cattle, and over all the earth, and over every creeping thing that creeps upon the earth" (Genesis 1:26). In this sense, man is *not like* the rest of nature; he is meant to govern the whole of it, and his first action is to echo what God himself has done, in *naming* creatures: "and whatever the man called every living creature, that was its name" (Genesis 2:19). And yet man is not created on his own special day. He is created on the sixth day, along with the cattle and the beasts of the earth, and the blessing he receives from God echoes the blessing God has given to the fish and the birds: "Be fruitful, and multiply" (Genesis 1:22, 28). The means by which we preserve the species is like what dogs and cats and cows and monkeys and deer and dolphins and pigs do, and that is one reason why we should not make sexual excitation into the leading motive of our existence. Dogs also scratch.

So let us consider the masculine creation that we may call the *team*.

Increasing and Multiplying

The first thing I want to note is that the team springs naturally both from the natural strength of the masculine and from its natural propensity for action in the world—both from the arm that can bend the bow and from the arrow of desire that makes a man want to bend it. Consider the economy of nature. It costs the species a lot more, in food and water, to make a male than to make a female. The benefit must then outweigh the cost. It would *not* outweigh the cost if each man and boy fended for himself, or if the men and boys were mixed indiscriminately with the women and the girls. In either case, most of the males' additional strength, and pretty much all of their drive to conquer, would be wasted or thwarted. There are all kinds of things you cannot do with babies and small children nearby—such as hunting dangerous or difficult game for the sake of the babies and the small children. These tend to be the same kinds of things you cannot do in tandem with creatures that do not possess the strength of full-grown men, and that rules out participation of the women and the young boys.

We do not simply want to *add together* the strength and the speed of, say, nine men on a baseball diamond, or a hundred men in a Roman military division, or twenty Iroquois men hunting elk. If you are gathering berries or roots, your actions are additive. Two people pick about twice as much as one person. Even the children can come along, and what they pick will top off the basket. But if you add to the Roman division twenty women who are no match for their own young sons in strength or speed, you do not get the division as it was and then some left over. You get confusion and breakdown. It is not just that a chain is only as strong as its weakest link. The male group is not like a chain. It is like a complicated machine or a body. Its actions, not by addition but by clever multiplication, give men the power to do things they could not even conceive of doing otherwise. Let me be precise here. If the job is to move a big rock weighing two tons, I can *conceive* of moving it, even though I know I cannot do it. All I need to think of is having the sufficient strength in my arms and legs. Maybe an elephant could make it budge. But hunting is not like that. It is *qualitatively* different. It cannot be done by adding. It can only be done if you make the leap, at once conceptual and social, from the individual—however strong and clever he could possibly be on his own—to the team.

Think of hunting bison. You do not just go after the animals, one man here and one man there. Your action must be coordinated. You are essentially fighting a war, using your brains to arrange the actions of men doing different things simultaneously. If it is winter, you may be surrounding the herd and using frightening noises to drive it onto a frozen lake, where the buffaloes' speed afoot will be useless, and you can kill them while they are vulnerable. If you are near a cliff, you can drive the herd toward its brink and frighten it right over the edge, killing dozens or hundreds at once. But to do either of these things, you must have a division of labor, and a plan, with the men doing different jobs, but with each job dependent upon the other jobs. Out of the individual strengths and wills of the different men, you must create a new thing, a hunting party, whose members at work are less like separate individuals than like the limbs of a body. When you see a group of boys playing touch football, with the quarterback tracing the next play on the palm of his hand as he and his teammates huddle saying, "Bobby, you start out right and cross over, like this, while you, Timmy, run out straight, and when Bobby crosses you, fake coming in and then go deep," you are witnessing an essentially masculine phenomenon, without which the human race could not have survived.

This is also how men multiply their strength with machines. The mind that conceives the hunting strategy and the football play also conceives the machine. In the case of the Indians hunting the bison, you had the machine of the bow and arrow, which again is a matter of the coordination of parts aimed at an end—not simply an addition of the characteristics of the parts, but a union that makes something entirely new, on a higher plane. What do you make the bow of? The wood must be able to be bent, but not too easily; the propulsive force comes not from the guiding string but from the bent wood that stores potential energy and seeks to return to its original shape. Will you be on horseback when you shoot? Then the bow must be shorter, because you will not have the leverage to draw a bow that is too long. What strings are best? What about the arrowhead? How do you keep the arrow from wobbling in flight or flittering off to the side? The flight of an arrow is like a football pass in this respect: it is most accurate if the arrow (or the ball) is spinning around its lengthwise axis, like a drill boring its way through the air. Think of the spinning of a bicycle's wheels that keeps the rider upright. Thus the Indians would fletch not only the back of the arrow's shaft but the arrowhead itself with bird feathers—to send the arrow spinning and keep it on target. Not any old feathers would do. The point, again, is not that each element is merely added to the other elements. You have to conceive of the arrow as a whole, or you never make a single advance.

Here I may seem to have left behind the masculine characteristics of strength and will to action, but it is not so. It is men's strength we are multiplying, not the strength of thirteen-year-old boys or women. The tools you create both assume the full strength of the man and require a man's strength to use. And, again, we are not talking about outliers. We are talking about such ordinary men as you can expect to find everywhere, with the strength they will have if they spend their hours outdoors, doing things.

Masculine Affection

The teams do not form in the abstract. They need the strong mortar of camaraderie, of masculine affection, which is not like what a man feels for a woman or what women feel for one another. The folktales of every culture in the world testify to it, so that when nature-haters in our time complain that our boys are taught (lamely, it appears, and inconsistently) to emulate heroes of strength and speed and courage and cunning, and that such a thing is arbitrary and could be otherwise, we might reply, "What have you got against the Sioux?" As they stammer, we might add, "What have you got against the Zulus?" And before they can answer, say, "What have you got against the Japanese? Who on earth are you to tell the Pacific Islanders that they should never have brought up their sons in the way they did, but rather in the way that you demand? What kind of cultural imperialists are you?"

No, it is not arbitrary. It is natural, and everywhere. Consider an Irish folktale about the Sons of Mor. The two elder sons have gone to seek their fortunes beyond the sea, in the Kingdom of the White Strand. The king keeps them there gladly because they are such grand champions. The youngest brother, left at home to protect his mother and provide for her, grows in strength and hardiness, wins the hand of a beautiful young woman in marriage—in tale after tale, it is the young hero who must win the fair maiden, *by victory in combat* or by perseverance at what seems an impossible task—and cannot rest until he finds his brothers. So he sails the seas and ends up in that same Kingdom of the White Strand. The king, observing the courage of the young stranger, does not dare to send his own men against him, but rather the two champions from far away.

So they wrestle. The eldest brother, dueling the young stranger, notices that he is better at giving knocks, and his opponent is better at turns and throws. And that is how the eldest recognizes the youngest, "for when we used to wrestle at home," he says, "I had the knocks and you had the turns." They embrace. Brothers wrestle with brothers. Or, the man with whom you wrestle is your brother.

That is the case with Young Conal in another Irish tale. Conal is in search of the wife who was stolen from him. He meets three champions who have set about the castle where Conal's wife is held captive. They do not know who Conal is, and he does not tell them that he is seeking his wife. The champions say they are in love with the woman, and that they can kill every other man who comes to the castle, but none of them can kill another of the three. So Conal fights them, killing two and overcoming the third, the Short Dun Champion. When Conal asks him if he has ever been nearer a fearful death than now, the Short Dun Champion tells his own story: in fact, a more fearful death did once face him, but he braved it by brains and stubbornness. Conal spares him, and they become more than friends. They become comrades: they plan the battle against the king and his castle together, and though Conal is the stronger of the two, he cannot prevail without the shrewdness of the Short Dun Champion. Conal wins—and gives the kingdom to his friend.

Something similar takes place between Gilgamesh and Enkidu, who wrestle with such force in the great square of Uruk that the city walls shake. Civilization itself hangs in the balance: Enkidu is a shaggy fellow from the wilds, not yet civilized; Gilgamesh is a brave king, two-thirds god and one-third man, but he has governed Uruk with arrogance. No young man is safe from being dragooned into his army, and no young woman is safe from his sexual advances or from being compelled to work in his household. When the people complain, the wise god Ea fashions Enkidu, a natural champion who lives like a wild beast among the other beasts until he is enticed by a temple prostitute and lies with her for seven days. When he rises up, he knows himself for a human being, and the beasts flee from him. The harlot says that he will know better things than drinking at the watering hole like the wild beasts. He will live in the city, and he will have the king as his fast friend.

Enkidu strides forth to challenge Gilgamesh, blocking the king's way to the house of a new bride, and the two fight like wild bulls. The pair wrestle, and Gilgamesh finally throws Enkidu, but when the match is over, the king is a new man. No one had ever challenged him so. From that moment on, the king and the wild man are the closest of friends, and Gilgamesh no longer oppresses his people. Instead, the two of them go forth into the mountains to slay Huwawa, the keeper of the great cedar forests. Cedar was the best building wood in those lands: think of Solomon, who "built the House of the Forest of Lebanon; its length was a hundred cubits, and its breadth was fifty cubits, and its height thirty cubits, and it was built upon three rows of cedar pillars, with cedar beams upon the pillars" (1 Kings 7:2). So what we have is male wildness and male arrogance transformed by the fight—by the brotherhood established in the fight—into a force for building civilization. There is no city without the brotherhood. It would never be built in the first place.

We go to the American Midwest. A new boy has arrived in town, wearing city finery, even shoes though it is only Friday. Another boy, Tom, sees him and is nettled:

> The more Tom stared at the splendid marvel, the higher
> he turned up his nose at his finery and the shabbier and

shabbier his own outfit seemed to him to grow. Neither boy spoke. If one moved, the other moved—but only side-wise, in a circle; they kept face to face and eye to eye all the time. Finally Tom said:

"I can lick you!"

"I'd like to see you try it."

"Well, I can do it."

"No you can't, either."

"Yes I can."

"No you can't."

"I can."

"You can't."

"Can!"

"Can't!"

Mark Twain has hit the bull's-eye. We see that as Tom Sawyer and the new boy prepare for a fight, they do so according to the immemorial rules of boyhood. Challenge leads to contradiction, which leads to insults back and forth, which lead to more chal-lenges, and then finally to the confrontation, "each with a foot placed at an angle as a brace, and both shoving with might and main, and glowering at each other with hate." That's a comic touch, that hate, because we sense that it is overdone, that the boys are playing a game deeply enjoyable to them both. At last, after a few more dares, they get to fighting in earnest,

rolling and tumbling in the dirt, gripped together like cats; and for the space of a minute they tugged and tore at each other's hair and clothes, punched and scratched each oth-er's nose, and covered themselves with dust and glory. Presently the confusion took form, and through the fog of battle Tom appeared, seated astride the new boy, and pounding him with his fists.

Boys play at opposition. It is agreeable to play at being disagreeable, to be *against* one another. Have we not heard the same strain a thousand times? "Get over here, you big lump of fat, so I can show you what a real fastball is like!" says a boy to his friend, grinning, and the friend replies, "With that noodle for an arm? My grandmother can throw a watermelon faster than you can throw a baseball!" And he pounds the dirt with his bat and takes a practice swing or two, gritting his teeth and narrowing his eyes. What fun it is to have an enemy you can trust! I know that, by emulation and imitation, women now form sports teams, but if anything is "socially constructed," it is that. It requires institutional encouragement, financial support, and reward in the form of generous college scholarships. For a very long time now, there have been girls' basketball teams, and yet you rarely see a group of girls spontaneously organizing themselves for a game on a basketball court or spontaneously organizing themselves for a pickup game of softball. Boys will invent more games in a year than girls have adopted from boys in fifty. It is in their nature to do so.

There are two reasons why the child-man engages in such behavior. One is obvious: to impress girls. The winner of a fight is covered with glory, and the girls are attracted to him, instinctively. He is strong and courageous; he can protect her and her children and provide for them. The quarterback does not go to the dance alone. But there is more to it than that. Again, we are social creatures. The winner will also be a leader among men. The woman who marries him need not fear that the others in the tribe or the town will combine against her and hers. She has caught the chief tiger by the tail. And still there is more. It is the second reason for such athletic feats, the reason that is not at all obvious to us now. It is to impress the other boys—not towards homosexual action, because that is a perversion of male friendship. Rather, we are dealing with the impetus to the bonds of brotherhood across bloodlines—a brotherhood that both transcends the family and protects all the individual families and clans that make up the city.

For that to happen, there must be a strong emotional pull, and one that does not really correspond with anything in a woman's experience, just as women's friendships do not really resemble those of men. How to explain it? Strength admires strength, cunning admires cunning. "In another world," says the defeated Romulan commander to Captain Kirk, "I might have called you friend." But women are not friends when their children hang in the balance; in fact they will often blame their husbands for *not* sticking up for their own, for compromising with the opposing family. When the female fights, she fights to the death. The male usually does not. A man will fight for the joy of the fight, because each fighter makes the other one stronger, and because the fight will establish a healthy and productive hierarchy, the soul of the team. The loser acknowledges the winner, the winner is gracious to the loser, and now they can go forth to get something done, something that requires both fraternity and hierarchy. Enkidu acknowledges the superiority of Gilgamesh, and Gilgamesh acknowledges the strength of Enkidu and profits from his good advice and his aid.

A Beneficial Hierarchy

The team is more than a group. It is a hierarchically organized social engine, embodying both the equality that is the foundation of brotherhood and the frank recognition of inequality that enables men to multiply their strength most efficiently and with greatest satisfaction.

The same sort of mind that makes complex machines that can function only by subordinating the action of some parts to others also forms teams and armies and construction crews and senates, composes and performs symphonies, and builds cathedrals. People living in complete security against the elements, with no fear of foreign invaders, and with no physically difficult or dangerous work to do from day to day can be complaisant as they decry hierarchy. Others may grudgingly admit that it is a necessary evil. But it is not. It is a positive good. It is the great multiplier. That men form hierarchies without embarrassment, and without necessarily destroying the real and important equality among them, is one of the most astonishing things we can say about them; it is something so common and so obvious that we do not even notice it. But I say: if you do not have hierarchy, you will not only fail at civilization, you will fail even to have a strong tribe of savages in the woods. You will not kill the bison.

Look at a football team. The eleven men on offense take instruction for the next play from the quarterback, the brain of their team. He in turn takes instruction from the offensive coordinator or from the head coach, either directly or indirectly. He calls the signals from the line of scrimmage and may change the play at will once he sees the formation of the defense, and then every player changes his own individual actions accordingly, because every one of them has in his mind and his muscles the memory of precise movements for each play in the playbook. On one play, the running back is not the center but rather, after faking to take the handoff from the quarterback, stays behind to block—to give up his body against a charging defensive lineman who so outweighs him that he will often run him over like a steamroller. On another play, the guards must "pull," requiring quick and sharp action, because the quarterback will be rolling out to the right for an "option," to pass to the wide receiver on that side or to keep the ball himself, and in either case the tight end, himself often a receiver of passes, will give up his body to block a defender a few yards downfield.

Everyone has a job to do, and it is essential to understand the character of the total thing. This is more than cooperation. It is more than sharing a general task. It is team action on another plane: the coordination of eleven movements to create a single movement that is other and more than the sum of the parts. It cannot be done without hierarchy.

Move from a football team to a building project. You are raising a cathedral in medieval France. From the very first, you meet with architectonic problems, questions of simultaneous coordination and subordination. The bishop gives the master builder his general instructions: it is to be a cathedral to the Blessed Virgin. That will imply hierarchy at every step. Practical and theological and liturgical concerns must all be orchestrated toward one grand common end. Because the church is to be filled with light, the stained-glass windows must be tall, taking up a large portion of the north and south walls. Because the walls will be pierced to provide space for the windows, the weight of the building must be buttressed from without. The buttresses must be planted in place and be surmounted by capitals, and perhaps there will be sculptures upon them too, like ornamental spikes. If there must be buttresses, they must be beautiful in their own right. Because the church is for the liturgy, there must be a large open space at the eastern end, where the priest will celebrate the Mass. The western facade, directed toward the setting sun, should depict events at the end of each human life and the end of the world and Christ as the final Judge of all. Which stained-glass windows should go where? Who decides? According to what plan?

The whole thing is like a musical composition. If each instrument were "equal"—playing the same note at the same time and with the same loudness and insistence—you would not have a symphony. You would not have anything meaningful. You would have a chaos of equality. Order implies subordination, hierarchy. So the master builder obeys and translates the desires of the bishop and his theological advisers into action, and the glaziers wait for the masons, and the masons, whose work is more important, still must wait upon the carpenters for scaffolding and for the great beams that will span the interior, and the carpenters not only give direction to but also heed the advice of men who scour the forests for the necessary timber. What the glaziers on the north wall are doing must be coordinated with and subordinated to what the glaziers on the south wall are doing, because the south is open to the afternoon sun (we are in the northern hemisphere), and thus should show the more important images. The team, which functions as a body made up of bodies, giving to each man the opportunity to work his skill, erects a building that is itself like the team that builds it.

Should some men govern others? What is the alternative? Should everyone have an equal say in what play will be called, at what angle the breakwater should be pitched when you dredge the harbor, what kind of stone should be set into the vaulted roof of the church, which recipe for concrete should be used for the piles you want to pound into the riverbed, and what should be the right tariff to balance the good of cheap prices against the good of protecting a fledgling industry at home—and on and on? As we can see immediately, the insistence upon equality in every respect and for every question overburdens the task and reduces the team to a gathering of squabblers. Eleven men on the offense may have eleven different opinions, and by the time you poll everyone, the game threatens to grind to a halt and the interest fades away. Or, if the men sense from the outset that there will be no leaders to follow but that everybody will have equal say in everything, they will never assemble to play the game. It would not be worth the trouble. Equality in every respect and for every question builds nothing. It cannot.

There is a concord between what builds and what is built. And any complex thing to be built *must* involve hierarchy, because its structure demands it: the walls hold up the roof, and the roof must be such as can be held up by the walls. The roof must span the interior space, and the quality of that space determines what sort of roof you must build. The space itself is determined by the use to which you wish to put it. If we are talking about a church, it is determined by the character of the sacred celebration: the assembling of a large number of people, their free movement, their orientation toward the sanctuary, the preaching of the word, and the conferring of the sacrament. Rules, everywhere—and the habit of mind which grasps that the interaction of the rules is in accord with the habit of the heart and the hands and the will that makes for the team and its network of rules and government.

You are at sea in a sailing ship. The web of masts, booms, spars, sails, and ropes is akin to the web of officers and men—the carpenters, rope-makers, sail-menders, the cook and the scullery boys, the mariners properly speaking. You may say that everyone depends upon the cook, and that would be true, or that everyone depends upon the captain, and that would be true in a different way, or that everyone depends upon the first mate or the boatswain who translates the captain's orders to the men, and that would also be true. Shakespeare shows us as much in the first scene of *The Tempest*, a scene that most critics have ignored, considering it as just a vehicle to introduce a few of the main characters and to have them stranded on an unknown isle. But it is a deft analysis of what a well-governed society looks like, a society governed by interwoven hierarchies.

The scene begins with thunder and lightning—quite an effect for the audience that has hardly found their seats in the theater! The Master calls to his second-in-command:

MASTER Boatswain!

BOATSWAIN Here, master. What cheer?

MASTER Good, speak to the mariners! Fall to it yarely, or we run ourselves aground. Bestir, bestir! *Exit. Enter* MARINERS.

BOATSWAIN Heigh, my hearts! Cheerly, cheerly, my hearts! Yare, yare! Take in the topsail! Tend to the master's whistle! Blow till thou burst thy wind, if room enough!

Leave it to Shakespeare to show us in just a few lines how hierarchy and equality *in certain respects* can be good friends indeed, and can get things done. The master is the master, and that is that. Yet, as we learn, he is *not* the chief personage aboard. That would be King Alonso of Naples, for whose sake the ship has been manned to go from Naples to Tunis and to return again. But during an emergency, everyone aboard ship, including the king, his brother, and their fellow aristocrats, must obey the master, which means they must obey the boatswain. The master assumes that the boatswain will obey him readily, and in fact that right-hand man is already at the master's elbow calling, "Here, master." The master addresses him affectionately but urgently, ordering him to "speak to the mariners" and to do things "yarely," meaning "on the spot," "readily," "promptly," implying that the mariners are also in position to obey, to do what needs to be done, immediately. If they do not, the ship will run aground, and that threatens to rip the hull out from below with the possible loss of every life aboard. Hence the *top*sail must be taken down. Notice: the highest of the sails, meant to catch a good wind on the open sea, is now a threat. The top must stoop to the bottom.

"Tend to the master's whistle!" cries the boatswain to the men, cheering them on. He does not call them "dogs" or "swabs," nor does he treat them as cogs in a machine. They are his "hearts," as we might say his "lads" or "boys." The whistle is interesting, too. The master cannot be everywhere, and in the roar of the storm and the sea his words would be lost anyway. He must give signals according to the patterns he whistles. Again we are in essentially masculine territory. The men on the field follow the commands called out on the bugle or the drum. The manager sends a message to the third-base coach, who relays it in signals to the batter, with a certain agreed-on signal being a meta-signal—a sign indicating that the next sign actually signifies, unlike the others, which are only distractions to fool the other team. The catcher sends signals to the pitcher, and the man on second base tries to steal them and relay them to his teammate in the batter's box. The language of hierarchy is often a language of symbols, which are ordered, higher and lower.

When the king and the aristocrats come on deck from below, they get in the way of the boatswain and his work:

ALONSO Good boatswain, have care. Where's the master? Play the men.

BOATSWAIN I pray now, keep below.

ANTONIO Where is the master, bos'n?

BOATSWAIN Do you not hear him? You mar our labor. Keep your cabins; you do assist the storm.

GONZALO Nay, good, be patient.

BOATSWAIN When the sea is. Hence! What cares these roarers for the name of king? To cabin! Silence! Trouble us not!

GONZALO Good, yet remember whom thou hast aboard.

BOATSWAIN None that I love more than myself. You are a councilor; if you can command these elements to silence and work the peace of the present, we will not hand a rope more. Use your authority. If you cannot, give thanks you have lived so long, and make yourself ready in your cabin for the mischance of the hour, if it so hap. Cheerly, good hearts! Out of our way, I say!

Alonso does go below, and the good old councilor Gonzalo heeds the boatswain's words, while the wicked Antonio and Sebastian stay above to curse the officer, to call him a dog and the son of a whore, and in general to *disobey* the law of right order, the hierarchy of obedience on the ship. Here *authority* is a good thing—authority distributed according to hierarchies that rightly depend on the differing needs of different places and times. The boatswain does not doubt Gonzalo's authority on land in keeping the peace. But aboard, in matters pertaining to the ship, the master, who is lower in the social scale, has the authority, and in this emergency the boatswain is invested with the authority of the master. And of course there is God above, the absolute master, whom all must obey, king and courtier and shipman alike.

You will notice that the boatswain speaks to the aristocrats with a remarkable bluntness and severity. The good Gonzalo takes it in

stride, jesting that their only hope is in the boatswain's looks: if ever
a man were destined to be hanged (rather than drowned), he is. But
Antonio and Sebastian, less manly by far, take the blunt speech as a
personal insult and hurl vicious insults back at the boatswain—getting
in the way of work to be done. I will have more to say about this
problem below.

But let us step back from the storm and look at the work of art it
begins. Which is the most important scene in *The Tempest*? You cannot say, "They are all equally important," because that is obviously
not true. The final scene, one of revelation, repentance, and redemp-
tion, is surely the scene that governs the eight scenes that precede it.
But the first scene sets forth the crucial questions that the play
addresses, and of course it tells us why the men are on the island, and
it gives them reason to suppose that they may be lost forever. Or is
the most important scene the penultimate one, a scene of trials surmounted and young married love? The point is not that you should
shrug and say that they are all the same, but that whatever equality
they possess is expressed in and through hierarchy.

Which is the most important piece on a chessboard? The queen is
the most powerful, but she serves the king and may be sacrificed to
win the game, while the king must be protected at all costs. The knight
is the least powerful of the major pieces, slightly less valuable than the
bishop, but the bishop is confined to the white squares or the black
squares, and the knight possesses the unique feature that when it
attacks any other piece besides another knight, the piece attacked cannot possibly be attacking it. The pawns are the weakest pieces, yet the
first great master of chess, Philidor, said that the game is won by their
play, and a king and a single pawn can win a game against a lone king,
while a king and a bishop or a king and a knight cannot do so.

Think now of the structures of government that men have
invented. In a world of pretended equality, brute strength or sheer

stubborn willfulness governs—which is to say that there is little government at all. The very word *government* derives from the language of the ship—ultimately from *kybernein*, the Greek word for steering a ship. Our word *cybernetics*, having to do with computer programming, implies hierarchies within hierarchies, nested or intertwining structures of command and obedience. When we are dealing with human beings, though, the structures most in accord with justice will take into account that the individual person, unlike a patch of code or a lever in a machine, is himself a center of inestimable worth. The best structures will thus make possible a hierarchically ordered liberty, which is good for all concerned, rather than the equalitarian license that looks like liberty but that very soon subjects everyone to the arbitrary dictates of whoever has the most muscle.

Consider the United States Constitution. What Madison and the other drafters of the Constitution wanted to establish was a kind of complex game of hierarchies. The president has the most power, and there are things that only he can do, but he cannot pass laws; his is the power to execute the laws that the people's representatives pass. The Senate is more stable than the House, and it has the authority to advise the president and approve or disapprove of his nominees to the Supreme Court, but the Senate cannot initiate legislation that requires the purse; only the House has that power. The Senate was also to be under the authority of the state legislatures, so that in this one very significant respect, the states held a hammer over the national government. The Supreme Court was to be the nation's final arbiter of cases at law, and, after the case of *Marbury vs. Madison*, it clearly had the authority to determine whether laws passed by Congress were in accord with the Constitution; but the Court could not legislate, nor could it command the executive on how to enforce the laws.

Much of the complexity of that game and its rules has been obliterated in the two centuries since the Constitution was adopted, both by the encroachments of the Court and by the unaccountable actions of federal departments nominally under the jurisdiction of Congress but actually behaving in independent and practically limitless and incomprehensible ways. It appears that men have retreated from the understanding that the rules of the game must be upheld lest, in a moment of sentimentality—which is often but power-grabbing with a peeled onion nearby to provide a few theatrical tears—good should be done to a limb or a cell at the expense of the body. No chess player can afford to have a favorite pawn. In time of war, no army general can afford to place any consideration for his troops above victory.

And we are now in a time when the threat of death by an infection far less deadly than the influenza that swept through the world in 1918—not to mention the surges of disease that beset Europe after the onslaught of the Black Plague in 1347 and then simmered, with many eruptions of virulence, for the next five hundred years—bids to sweep away the whole game of ordered liberty. We cannot have a conversation about how we are to live, if we will not accept the risk of death. We will not have that conversation, if those who try to begin it are cowed into silence by accusations that they are killers.

Masculine, for What Purpose?

Feminists show little willingness to consider that before men created the high technological world they take for granted, the overriding concern of most people at most places was how to survive from one year to the next and, if possible, to live with some modest comforts and nourishment for the soul. It is as if a woman in 1860 could light a fire with as much unconcern and as little intelligent preparation as you need when you turn on a light bulb, or prepare a single meal without bringing to bear a whole host of forgotten skills, not to mention the sheer miserable hard work of "slaving over a hot stove."

When my own grandmother, who in her very advanced old age was beginning to lose her grip on things, was asked for her recipe for chicken soup, she replied, "First you have to pluck the chicken." She actually used a colorful adjective to describe the chicken, or rather the annoyance of having to pluck it. Imagine you are living a hundred years ago. You surely cannot afford to buy new clothes every year, even if there is a shop selling such things in your town. So you had better be good with the needle. What if you want to enjoy year-round the vitamins in strawberries or peaches or some other fruit that is ripe for only a few weeks of the year? How do you do that? You have to have the equipment—and the know-how—to can fruits and vegetables without putting your family at risk of botulism.

Your husband has plenty of work to do also. Much of that work resides squarely in a man-made "world" of men: in the quarries, offshore in a fishing boat, in the fields, in the woods with a lumbering crew, among a party of hunters, upon the scaffolding of a building rising from the earth, and so on. It is natural for men to form these teams of work, as I have said—it is in the blood. Thus it is also natural for men to form those games of government that control and direct the actions of those teams beneath them. No one ever thought otherwise. It no more occurred either to men or to women that women should be senators than that they should be warriors, merchants on the ocean, builders of great public works, or members of any other team aimed at accomplishing something requiring the coordinated strengths of many men, often at immediate risk to life and limb. The actions of virtuous and even half-decent men are *for all the people*, and most centrally for the women and the children. The women and the children are primary in the order of ends, and he is secondary and ancillary. They are indispensable, and he is indispensably dispensable: it is his great virtue and honor to pour out his sweat and his blood for their sake.

We may turn the question around and ask whether when women enter politics they place a priority on the interests of men as a group, or whether they even have such interests in mind. I am not represented by a member of my race or sex or ethnicity. I am represented by someone who takes my part, or who at least considers me. But if it is not natural for a woman to want to protect men, aside from her own husband and sons—and the feminist insistence that women be placed into combat is most telling, as if a few extra dead or crippled men, not to mention the women themselves, were a small price to pay for the fantasy of sexual indifference—then men should not expect women to represent them. The feminists are thus caught in a bind. The good man can naturally express his manhood by putting women and children first. But to do the like, the feminist must virtually give up her feminism.

My point here is that men have nothing to apologize for. It is assumed that the only reason why women were not permitted to hold a place in the parliaments or senates of the world, anywhere, was that men simply desired to keep them down. But to make this assumption is to fail to acknowledge the inescapable necessities of life before our age, and to fail to understand that men, in their teams, in their councils, *created those very institutions of government in the first place*, and our first question should not be why they did not permit women to take part in them, but why they would trouble to create such things at all. Mariana Griswold van Rensselaer—a formidable woman, an accomplished author on sacred and secular architecture in Europe and the United States, a great patroness of the arts, and a leader in the *anti-suffrage* movement—in her 1894 pamphlet *Should We Ask for the Suffrage?* asked the obvious question: *Why* is it *men* that make governments?

"Man's greater physical strength," she says, "is not merely a reason why he has hitherto done all the work of government. It is also a sign and proof that this is part of his natural work. By nature he is the protector of his family . . . whether it be attacked by wolves, by human individuals, by the fear of poverty, or by the dread of public calamities. And by nature a woman is a being to be protected. Her physical weakness is a sign of this." Mrs. Van Rensselaer saw that the best arrangement would encourage both men and women to do their particular work most conscientiously, in harmony with one another, rather than have women assume half of the job of home-protecting and men half of the job of home-keeping, with each sex acting athwart its nature and therefore performing the work rather poorly, and adding to the confusion ingratitude and a mutual distrust between the sexes.

"If you think I am thus assigning an 'inferior' role to women," she says, expressing the insight that a hierarchy in one respect may be reversed by a hierarchy in another respect, "you have very little idea of relative values. You do not say that the bird on her nest plays an inferior role while her mate brings her food, fights off her enemies, and sings for her pleasure." Think what exertions a boy will make, what crazy stunts, to attract a girl's attention, even just to make her laugh. Write those exertions large. "It is simply and solely for the safeguarding of the home, and of woman as the centre of the home, that government exists, that men labor and fight and strive and try to rule. Fancy a nation composed only of men—how long do you think they would care how it was governed?" Not long. What would be the point?

What Mrs. Van Rensselaer saw, and what was actually the focus of the debate at the time, was that to expand the vote beyond male suffrage was, in effect, to replace *the household* as the fundamental political unit with *the individual*. That would be a seismic shift. Many a progressive author at the time was opposed to it—and not because they had a low view of women. Certainly William Gladstone, the great Liberal prime minister of England, did not. When the issue finally came to a head, and at a time when he could have used the additional votes, he backed away from his former support for women's suffrage, saying that he was wary of intruding politics into the sacred realm of hearth and home. Life was already being reduced to the actions of unattached human atoms of will and desire; the novels of Charles Dickens are full of pictures of what happens when institutions such as businesses and governments view men and women as mere individuals and not *as members of a household*, actual or potential. In *Hard Times*, the workers of Coketown are submerged below individuality: they are mere "hands." The worst sin of Ebenezer Scrooge in *A Christmas Carol* is not his avarice, which is great, but his sub-humanity, his refusal to see human beings as involved with one another. Bob Cratchit, his clerk, is a mere employee—Scrooge knows nothing about Cratchit's family, nor does he want to know. The last thing that Western men needed at the time was *more* encouragement to see life as the pursuit of individual gain—to thrust the household from its central place.

We see that there is a way to look at the male-only institutions of the past as neither invidious nor oppressive of women, but as a natural expression of the masculine imperative that Mrs. Van Rensselaer observed: men labor and fight and strive so that there may be decent homes and villages and cities, so that there may be feasts and religious celebrations, so that children will grow up healthy and sane and the next generation will be able to provide for the well-being of the people in the future. We are perhaps deceived by the historian's predictable and understandable focus on wars and migrations and discoveries into overlooking the fact that, even in a military empire such as Rome, most people at most times and places are engaged in the affairs of an orderly and ordinary life. You are a woman living in Florence in 1600. It is November, and you are wearing a woolen coat to keep warm. The wool for your coat came from sheep in England. It was sent in raw form to Flanders, where it was worked into cloth—and not for the fun of it, for money. The gold and silver ore—because you need something that is both stable and valuable everywhere to serve for currency—had to be gotten from the earth by men going down the mines. It had to be tried by fire and purified in a foundry. It had to be transported by ship or by overland caravans. It had to be punched into coins. All to allow that woolen cloth to be brought from Flanders to Florence to be dyed, in trade, for money. The dyes must also be manufactured. And the Florentines do not dye cloth for the fun of it, either. Most of that now fully finished cloth will be traded for spices and drugs and other goods from the East, overland or by ship. Who builds the ships? Who hews the timber for the masts and the planks? Who sails the ships? Who protects them from privateers?

What is it all for? Would men do these things for themselves? Men would rather live hand to mouth out in the wilds.

The miracle of culture and of civilization is the miracle of the transformation and redirection of masculine energy from the willful self to the team, the work crew, the school, and the army—for the sake of the home and the women at the center of the home, and, in the end, for the sake of the city and the nation. But this miracle does not occur unless it springs from and fulfills certain passions in the boy and the man. You do not make teams happen just by persuading men that it would be useful to have them. You have them because men *enjoy them*, they are attracted to them, they build men's muscles, train their wills, and sharpen their minds.

Think of the Greek boy going to the *gymnasion* to learn to sing the poems of Hesiod and Homer, to read and reckon, and to train the body so that it will be fit for the citizen-soldier he is to be. We must not be so obtuse as to say that girls *were not permitted* to go there, to wrestle naked with the naked boys, so that eventually they

could become—what? No one gave that possibility a thought. Forming such a thing as a school is simply one of the things that men do,
just as they form armies, oriented not toward their good as a sex apart
from women—for there is no such thing, as the interests of men and
women are inextricably entwined with one another—but toward the
common good. When, however, technology and industry had
advanced to such a point as to make it both feasible and profitable
for girls to be educated along with their brothers, that is what men
did, and it required no great persuasion for them to do it.

No apologies, then, for the masculine institutions of the past.
Instead, we should question our refusing to grant to men and boys
the opportunity or even the legal permission to form groups that are
natural to them and that have proved to be so marvelously productive. I am not going to prescribe for every man and woman what
groups they may or may not join. But what if something of that masculine conflict, that dynamic enmity, that sharpening of opponent
against opponent and friend against friend, that bold affirmation of
equality within hierarchy, and that readiness of equals to form and
to submit to hierarchies is dissipated in the company of girls and
women, so that the groups no longer accomplish all that they might?
What if the sign on the tree house, No Girls Allowed, is not meant
so much to keep girls away but to protect the male friendships from
having to compete with eros—to attract the boys to male teams and
to keep them in, ultimately for the good of the women that those
same girls will become?

Think, think. Roman Catholics have abundant experience of
what happened when girls were permitted to serve at the altar. The
boys disappeared. Why? No doubt for a variety of coinciding reasons,
most of which the boys themselves would have been hard put to
describe. The camaraderie was spoiled. The older boys, instead of
being rather like the first mate or the master-at-arms aboard a ship,

instructing the smaller boys in what to do and how to do it, would now stick out and look absurd. The priests themselves lost interest in what had been the church's most obvious source of vocations to the priesthood. What the servers were expected to do was less and less, till finally in many a parish they are little more than cute decorations in pajamas. Nobody, not even the women who pressed for altar girls, thinks of them as essential, or as soldiers of Christ in training. It is not just that boys find it repugnant to be decorative, to be observed as being pretty. It is that the whole deal ceases to be inspiring or interesting. Thus do boys largely accept the sexual indifference that their elders preach to them, but they behave as anyone with any knowledge of the creature would have predicted. They may indeed say that there should be women priests. They will say so as they stay home on Sunday, playing video games.

If it is objected that the all-male group doing public business is a violation of the American Constitution or of fundamental justice, I have three answers. The first is to ask what has happened to *freedom of association*. It is natural for human beings to come together in groups in pursuit of the common good. Neither women's clubs nor men's clubs need any justifying. It is enough that the sexes enjoy sometimes being by themselves, and that they do things in those groups that they would not do otherwise, or would not do in the same way or as well, or would not derive the same satisfaction from doing. I do not see why we should draw a sharp distinction in this regard between the Shriners and the machine shop next door. If the head of a business wants to hire only men or only women, his or her decision is either well-founded or not. If it is not, the business suffers for it in competition with others, in which case laws forbidding this expression of associative freedom are unnecessary. If it is well-founded, then it is flatly unjust to forbid the single-sex business by law or even to subject the owner to moral opprobrium.

My second point in reply is that in fact there is good reason to suppose that the synergy, the friendly rivalries, the ease, the dash of the all-male group can make it tremendously productive. Think of the most brilliant animated cartoons that Americans have known, coming from a free-speaking and rowdy male enclave at Warner Brothers, with Tex Avery, Friz Freleng, Bob Clampett, Robert McKimson, the composer Carl Stalling, the man of a thousand voices Mel Blanc, and that ever-boyish maker of devilry Chuck Jones. What have we had since their heyday that is fit to clean their spittoons? Let them be. So long as there are plenty of opportunities for women to have their own groups or to join the great majority of groups that are open to both sexes, we have no cause to want to shut the men down. For what purpose? Where is the champion of human diversity when you need him?

Third, I will note that we have businesses and publicly financed groups that are all-female by rule, and no one objects. That is, we have women's sports. What we derive from them that is a boon to our culture, I do not know. Of course, if men or even teenage boys were permitted to try out for the LPGA or the WNBA, that would be the end of those leagues. But that is neither here nor there. If it is all right—indeed, if it is commanded—that a school district should spend a good deal of money on girls' sports, with rather little community interest, for a middling sort of athletic result, then surely it should be permissible for men, costing nobody anything, to unite in groups to do scientific work, or to build bridges, or to draw cartoons—whatever they like. That is liberty, and it redounds to the common good.

So we should not apologize for the all-male Renaissance studios that produced Michelangelo, Raphael, Titian, Tintoretto, and thousands of artists all over Europe in an age of unparalleled creativity and dynamism. What have our art studios done that is remotely

comparable? The results, if nothing else, more than justify the institutions. We need not call for a strict separation of the sexes in all
schools and in all businesses. No one really wants such a thing. But
we also need not and should not submit to the demand that all
schools and all institutions established for the advance of culture, the
protection of the nation, and the promotion of the common good be
open always to both sexes alike. I prefer to have Michelangelo.

The Missing Icon: Brotherhood

So far, I have justified the male group with appeals to practicality:
what it accomplishes. Let me stress again that there can be severance
of what works from what pleases. If it is good for society (and particularly for women and children) that men form teams, it is also
good *for the men*: it expresses and satisfies a deep desire and helps to
bring men out of themselves.

Unless men unite in groups to protect the tribe or the city, there
will soon be no tribe or city to protect. And they will not unite in
those groups if not for the bonds of strong feeling. Women make
friends more readily than men do, and perhaps for that very reason
they do not feel the need to forge friendships in the context of a group
that is more important than the particular persons who make it up.
If food is readily available to pick in the wild, you do not need to
farm. As always with us finite and embodied persons, what is a
strength in one respect is a shortcoming in another, and what is a
shortcoming in one respect is a strength in another. We need a great
force to overcome the natural male antagonism and aloofness. That
force may be found in the male admiration of the hero, who unites
the individual boys and men in *brotherhood*.

Again we are talking about what is universal to all cultures. I will
take one brotherhood as paradigmatic of the rest.

We are at the Sea of Galilee. Some men are in their boats, mending the nets. They are the brothers Simon and Andrew, and the brothers James and John with their father Zebedee. Jesus approaches the shore. He says, "Come, follow me, and I will make you fishers of men" (Matthew 4:19). No sooner said than done. They follow. Some months later, with crowds following along, he passes by the house of a tax farmer. For that is how the Romans got the funds to finance their armies and their public works. They employed people who were told to get a certain sum from a certain territory, letting them keep whatever remained over, so that it was the tax farmer's livelihood to squeeze the people, because otherwise he himself would be responsible for the bill. Thus were the tax farmers hated, especially by the Jews, who considered them as traitors to their nation. But Jesus says to Matthew the tax farmer, "Follow me," and Matthew, probably to the disgust of many among the crowd, does so. The hero calls, and the man responds.

This is and is not miraculous. It is, because there appears to be no reason why anyone would follow Jesus, since he is not Alexander or Caesar or Plato or Aristotle; he has as yet done little in the eyes of the world. It is not miraculous, that is, it is not something that surprises us, because it is exactly the kind of thing that men in groups do. They incorporate themselves. They agree to be led by the leader, because they see in him something good and heroic, something beyond themselves. The leader raises them up.

That such groups among human sinners can turn to evil is neither here nor there. All powerfully good things can be abused, and the better a thing is, the worse it becomes when it is corrupted. A bad dog is worse than a bad pig, a bad man is worse than a bad dog, and a bad angel is worse than a bad man. And we are going to have the male groups whether we like them or not. One name for them is the gang. The question is not whether to have them, but which ones to foster.

Jesus chose twelve men to be his apostles, his band of brothers. I have heard it said that Jesus did so only because it was what the people around him expected. I find that objection to be absurd. When did Jesus ever bow to mere convention? What might he have feared, that they would crucify him? Christians believe him to be the son of God, and if that is so, why, the son of God may do as he pleases. I have then heard it said that Jesus knew that the people of his time were not ready, say, for female priests, so that his choosing only men to be his apostles was an act of mercy for the poor ignorant people roundabout. But this objection also does not work. Priestesses were all over the place in the Mediterranean world; the Jews were a notable exception. And again, we presume that one who could raise the dead could do something a lot less remarkable, such as moving the hearts of men to accept a woman as the head of a congregation.

I believe rather that Jesus chose twelve men because it was the right thing to do, simply. And we can understand this in several ways. First, he wanted these men to go forth and conquer the world, baptizing all nations. That is, he was forming an army. Such an intention is implicit in what he says to Simon when he "baptizes" him as Peter, "and on this rock I will build my church, and the gates of Hades shall not prevail against it" (Matthew 16:18). Gates prevail by resisting the battery of an invading army set to crush them. The church therefore is meant to be on the offense. Men form armies. The physical capability is at one with the passion for doing so.

That implies a second way to understand it. Men followed Jesus, bound to him in that peculiar form of love called brotherhood. Jesus was a man, and he too, as a man, felt what other men feel. To say "Jesus should not have chosen twelve men to be his apostles" is to say "Jesus should have left this natural and culturally creative passion to be idle." But why? A given man here or there may choose not to marry. But no society can survive if most men do so. Presumably such a man gives up that kind of love for the sake of an even greater love. There must be a reason. Political correctness is no reason for Jesus to have forgone the brotherhood. And Jesus was notably friendly to women and gentle with them. He had a manly protectiveness toward the sex, which by no means did he always show to men. We cannot imagine Jesus crying out against women as he did against the Pharisees, calling them a brood of vipers. Yet this same Jesus chose twelve men to be his apostles.

"But it was only men who said so!" That objection holds no force. It insinuates that the apostles were liars. But why would they suppress the existence of some female apostle, when they put forth the holy women as the first witnesses to the Resurrection? Why would Luke drop the name of a woman apostle from the list, when he makes such a great point of exalting Mary, not Joseph? And why should we trust the apostles and the evangelists in the great matter of the Resurrection, when we reject them in a relatively small thing such as this?

But let us look more closely at this band of brothers. It is the platoon, the football team, the hunting party, the construction crew, the sailors at sea. It is not a mere collection. It embodies both equality and hierarchy. Jesus does not like Peter the best of all. He is friendliest with John, the brother of James. But he names Peter as the chief. In all the lists of the apostles, Peter's name comes first. And Peter, James, and John are separated sometimes from the rest. They alone, not all of the twelve, are with Jesus on the mount of Transfiguration. They alone are with Jesus in Gethsemane. They alone are with him when he enters the home of the chief of the synagogue, whose daughter has apparently died, and "he allowed no one to follow him" otherwise (Mark 5:37). Jesus sent seventy men forth to preach; twelve men were his intimate friends; three of those he selected from the rest for special revelations or for his own comfort in his agony in the garden, and one of those three, and not the one he liked the best, he chose to be the chief of the rest. "Feed my sheep," he says to Peter, and all of the apostles look to Peter as their head.

This is all masculine behavior—and God has blessed it. Far be it from us to set it aside.

A Change in Essence?

I think that most sensible people will admit that if you bring girls into a troop of Boy Scouts, the troop changes. It is not just that the girls will want to do things that the boys do not want to do, but that the boys lose some of what made the Scouts appealing, and they refrain from doing what otherwise they might do, because it doesn't work with girls in their midst. The feminist lawyer who sued The Citadel so that the school would admit women confessed as much in a burst of breathless honesty, saying that the Citadel experience would be changed utterly. If that is so, then surely it is admissible for us to ask whether the change is for the better or whether the change, even if it should result in something good, has come at the cost of something very different that was also good, and perhaps necessary or in danger of dying away.

I have spoken much about the team, and not so much about what I like to call *dynamic enmity*, something that characterizes masculine politics. Women have sometimes expressed amazement, even dismay, that a male defense attorney and the male prosecutor in a homicide case can pummel each other about the ears for two weeks and then go to the tavern for a steak dinner and drinks. Here again we witness the masculine capacity to set things in proper emotional compartments, to bracket, to feel and express great passion at one moment and then to set it aside as if it were irrelevant. And in fact most passion is irrelevant in some respect or other. Your legitimate scorn for Mr. Jones will get in the way today when he proposes a measure that will genuinely redound for the common good. Your duty is to set that scorn aside.

There is more. You cannot fight with your pinky extended. Fights are bloody. To play football, as I have said, you have somehow to enjoy *being tackled, being bruised*. You cannot be solicitous for your flesh. Politics is a blood sport. It must be. Too many questions of great moment are involved, even questions of the life and death of persons, the thriving or the dying of a culture or a nation. What we need is dispassionate passion, a willingness to wrestle, to beat the opponent bloody or to be beaten bloody ourselves, *and then to move on*, rather than retire to a closet, weeping. So we may legitimately ask whether that is what women who enter politics want. Etiquette here is deadening and dangerous, because it may prevent necessary conversations and arguments from occurring at all.

The entry of women into politics, as I observe it at least, has not had the ennobling and elevating influence that the early feminists promised: that women would help to civilize men and thus avert the bitter conflicts of civil and international war, and that discussions in legislatures would be less likely to degenerate into angry outbursts; niceness would be all in all. That has not happened. Politics is as bloody as ever, and in one important respect it is bloodier than it ever was before. When only the men were involved in political controversy, it was useful to have half of the rational adult population *not involved*, not embroiled, so as to protect the realm of personal life that political life should serve. But politics now takes Solomon's sword and divides the baby in half, with the women looking on in implacable ferocity and the men taking their stand to protect one woman or the other. Politics has not made women more like men, but it has rewarded the shrew at the expense of the lady, and it has short-circuited the dynamism of the duel of men against men in the arena. The prime directive is still and always to protect the woman, and not to play football.

We have great problems to address. Take one of them: the possibility that human activity is having a considerable and baleful influence upon the earth's climate, with disastrous effects to ensue. I do
not believe that claim, but I understand that my belief is not dispositive. The evidence must be examined with energetic care, but it
must also be examined with a cold dispassion. We require both at
once, and even from the same person. An issue like this must not be
decided by our personal beliefs or preferences. But we also can't let
ourselves be rushed into ruining economies for the sake of what is
still a heap of guesses upon guesses: not just that the earth is growing
warm, but that the responsibility for the warming lies mainly with
man, that the warmth will be catastrophic, that man can do something about it, and that this cure will not be worse than the disease.
Yet we will not have the spirited and dynamic discussion that would
help us decide these questions. We cannot have it. Let the teenage
scold Greta Thunberg, scowling and pointing her skinny finger at the
world, crying "How dare you!" stand as the poster girl. In a sane
world, her mother would have taken her aside and said, "My dear,
this is not for you. You do not know what you are talking about. You
are not a scientist." In a sane world, the men might have smiled and
said, "Young lady, your shrieking does not help. We have work to do,
and you are getting in the way." But instead, the visceral demand took
over: to round the wagons and keep the women and children inside,
protected—only now it is the women's and children's personal and
very emotional opinions that are protected on the stage of public
debate, where protection of those opinions at all costs may be at odds
with the common good.

Take another problem: the collapse of the black family in the
United States. We see immediately that any frank analysis of the
trouble must necessarily be acutely painful to many people. Single
mothers, after all, are everywhere. Their sons, who want to protect

them and defend them from all blame, are everywhere. The men who fathered the children and then went their way are everywhere. And I do not limit myself here to one race. One leg is full of blood poisoning, but the other leg is red and swollen and looking pretty angry too. The trouble is endemic. Suppose you have an assembly of men alone. Some of them have fathered children out of wedlock. Can the hard and bitter and intensely dispassionate discussion occur? Yes, it can. It is by no means inevitable; you have no guarantee; the esteemed senator may take a cane to the head of his esteemed colleague. But it can occur. Put ten or twelve women in that assembly who are or who have been single mothers, or who have daughters that are, and you will probably not get the two senators at each other's throats, but you will also not get the discussion. "How dare you!"

Politics is often a tragic endeavor, and economics a dismal science. Whatever solution you may propose for a widespread or deeply entrenched problem *must hurt many people.* There is no way around it. We have, in 2020 and 2021, been in the midst of a pandemic. In no Western nation have I witnessed any of the hard discussions that should have taken place between the guardians of public health, the guardians of economic welfare, the guardians of social life, and the far-sighted statesmen who might see where bad precedents might lead. I am not saying here that the nations did the wrong thing by enforcing lockdowns for many months on end. I am making no epidemiological claim at all. I am saying rather that men did not behave as men are wont to do, in part because of the essential change in political bodies, where everyone senses that protection at all costs, rather than the good and bloody battle, is the rule of the day. As soon as someone says, "You want 200,000 people to die," the chance for a discussion is over, because the rejoinder, "You are speaking like a coward and an ass," is no longer possible.

Our schools are in desperate need of reform. It will not happen, because any reform must be bloody and painful, and people in charge must be willing to accept a great measure of blame without taking things personally. No man can now stand up before the head of a school board and say, "A drag queen giving a lecture to small children? Mike, what were you thinking? Are you out of your mind?" And the sense that no such frank and cold-eyed man will be permitted to say such a thing gives irresponsible people much room for mischief.

Our public morals are a shambles. Only drastic reform would fix things, and it will not happen, because the potential reformer knows at the outset that he will be accused of hatefulness—of wanting certain sexually confused people to suffer and die. No, these things will not get done. Men and women are, in different ways, both to blame. But until our political bodies as they are currently constituted show that they can get any serious work done, rather than being neutered at the outset when any crucial question arises or collapsing in a fury of personal affront, I say that men should not apologize one bit for the all-male character of senates and congresses of the past. I want results.

CHAPTER FOUR

The Family

"Write in Civile this I finde:
Thogh it be noght the houndes kinde
To ete chaf, yit wol he werne
An Oxe which cometh to the berne,
Thereof to taken eny fode.
And thus, who that it understode,
It stant of love in many place:
Who that is out of loves grace
And may himselven noght availe,
He wolde an other scholde faile."

—John Gower, *Confessio Amantis*, 2.83–93

"I find this written in Justinian's code: Though it is not
in the dog's nature to eat hay, yet will he get in the way
of an ox that comes to the barn to take his feed. And
so too, let him understand it who may, does the same
motive apply to love: whoever is out of love's favor and
can do nothing to help himself, wishes that the other
man should fail also."

Beware of the vice of envy. It is the only one of the seven deadly sins that brings not even the simulacrum of a pleasure. Pride may get things done. You may, like Augustus Caesar, want to find your city in brick so that you can leave it in marble. It will not please God, this all too human pride, but at least Rome will shine in the sun after a rainstorm, not look like heaps of mud. Lust may revel in the beauty of the human body. Even sloth may once in a while enjoy doing nothing on a pleasant afternoon. But envy is always looking cross-eyed—that is what the Latin *invidia* means—at something good that someone else enjoys, and wishing to ruin the enjoyment. It is spiritual poison for weaklings.

Specifically, envy is the spiritual poison for feminists who see what healthy men and women enjoy, do not themselves enjoy it, and therefore want to ruin it for everyone else. We can see this in academe. Feminist scholars have discovered no neglected female Chaucer, so they must tear the actual Chaucer down and make sure that nobody else learns from him, calling him a racist and a rapist and whatnot. They cannot of themselves produce a Shakespeare, so they must tear him down or wrench his meaning away from the Christian faith he so often portrays in dramatic action. And on it goes. They have discovered no neglected female Titian, no neglected female Bach. There are none to discover. Should there be? Why, when these are already the rarest of men? Is it a slight against the rest of us men who are not Titian or Bach that such men have existed? We have long known about great authors such as Jane Austen. We have known about the painter Mary Cassatt and about Nadia Boulanger, the instructor of composers. We did not need feminism for that. So the weak woman—not the strong woman!—turns with a sour eye against a greatness she can neither attain nor love. Weak men would do the same, but they would be ashamed to confess to it in the presence of other men.

And this same envy explains the hatred of the natural family. It is not hard to figure.

Male Domination and Patriarchy

If you walk down the street of any city of the world where family life has broken down, you will be in danger from unattached and irresponsible males. That is inevitable. Boys without fathers may be less manly than boys with fathers, but they may well be more aggressive in unhelpful ways, more likely to express their need for risk and action as against a stifling life of women—mother, teachers, social workers—everywhere. The boys will seldom say that they have anything against those women. They have derived their only sustenance from them. They will feel grateful, sort of, and protective, sort of. They may even have learned the alphabet of feminism. Talk to men in prison, and they will tell you about their distant and worthless fathers in accents to make the sullen woman's heart flutter. Let them believe and profess what they may, but none of it matters in the end. Nature will have her revenge. The boy born with a sweet temperament, the boy who was always kind to his mother but who has lacked the ordering discipline and direction of the father, will get his girlfriend pregnant, attach himself to the questionable entrepreneur on the street corner, look with admiration on the restless and the bold, furnish himself with a gun—for the fun of it, not for any malice—and he is one bad choice or one stroke of bad luck away from death or a prison. He can be amiable and thoroughly antisocial at once. At the best, his energy is squandered.

That is *male domination*, as distinct from patriarchy. And it is not pretty. That boy is going to be stronger than his sister, whether he has a father in the home or not. He is going to be more attracted to danger than his mother is, no matter what she says, and in fact, the typical boy is likely to resent his mother's care and want to shrug it away, so that the more she harps on his risky behavior, without any strength to enforce her commands, the more he will doubt the justice of the commands themselves. He will think that she wants him to be like her not for his sake but for hers, and he will not want to comply. For whether she likes it or not, he will have that masculine propensity to set feelings apart from thoughts, and he will say to himself, "Her feelings aren't what is real." She may have the money, she may cook his meals, she may appeal to that irregular and unreliable thing called the heart, but he will hold the hammer.

The point is that patriarchy—government by fathers—is a victory over the male domination and the male irresponsibility you inevitably get when women attempt to take over male executive roles. When the patriarchs are missing, what you get from the boys is either aggressive disobedience or underachievement and waste. And then you get unhappy girls who despise the boys they have helped to form. The girls, too, go bad, because the sexes are made for each other, and you cannot corrupt one without corrupting both. If feminism has brought joy to the world, where is it? Where are the mirthful equality and the child-rich families of women liberated from womanhood and men liberated from manhood? Where are the beautiful works of art and music they have produced? Where are the bold and confident people who can take on opponents with grace and kindly laughter? What have we as a civilization gotten from them, besides bumper stickers and T-shirts? If women lead men, where are the happy female bosses—and the joyful men they lead? If feminists are good for boys, where are the boy geniuses fostered by feminists? Why do people in an egalitarian wonderland not sing their love of the sexes? The truth is, as C. S. Lewis says, that love does not speak the language of equality. It speaks the language of gratitude and superiority, of awe at the unique characteristics that make the beloved different from oneself. Dante did not fall in love with Beatrice because she was his equal.

When fathers go absent, do not expect women to take their place. That is not possible. Individuals may do the best they can, but we have laws and customs for the generality, not for the exception. Societies dominated by women tend to be insecure. My mother and a girlfriend could walk down the streets of her hometown with confidence, even after dark. Men might whistle at her, but she did not feel it as an assault—nor was it intended that way. She was confident. She could be confident, because fathers (and big brothers) were everywhere, and they kept order. She was not saddled with the burden of feeling that every notice of her beauty was aggressive and dangerous (as it now may well be). Because she felt safe, because in fact she was safe, she did not need to cry out for a "safe space." I am not saying that bad things never happened in those days. We are talking about the atmosphere, good and breathable, though lightning might strike in a storm—as opposed to the current brew that swelters with gaseous methane and ammonia, fairly prickling with electricity.

Fatherhood *makes for a productive kind of safety*. There is a reason why a woman can travel in Italy and be secure in her person, if not in her belongings. "You must not strike a woman, not even with a flower," says an Italian proverb (while of course you may beat another man to a bloody pulp, if necessary). This proverb would be just an idle sentiment were it not for the steely wills of the men backing it up. You do not touch that woman, because she has a father and brothers and uncles. You do not rape that woman, unless you want to wake up in a ditch the next morning bleeding from the crotch. The deterrent works. It is enshrined in the minds of boys and men, who naturally want to be protectors of those they love, and not mere predators on those they do not love.

Watch a father playing with his small child. There are things he can do that the mother either cannot do or would not try to do. He tosses the child in the air and catches him. He swings the child around like an airplane. I used to stand my son in front of me and tell him to grab me by the thumbs, and then I would raise my arms straight over my head, so that he went up in the air too, holding on tight and laughing. All of that is to say, "The world is a dangerous place, but the danger is good, and we are stronger than it. There is nothing to be afraid of." Consider the difference between "city officials" and "city fathers." A city official can be the enemy of the most human things in life. The official abstracts himself from the persons he governs. He is padded around with the comfortable fat of officialdom, of indirection, of bureaucracy. But the city father is not so. The father is one with the citizens he governs in flesh and blood, in aspiration and delight, in watchful care and in striving toward a noble end. He does not want them to remain little children or to be mere subjects of regulation. He wants them to be grown-up and strong, energetic and confident. He will make others safe in part by demanding no safety at all for himself. That is what fathers do. What do men who fail or refuse fatherhood do? They dissipate their strength in empty pursuits, or they make others insecure for their own power and pleasure—making for a world where it is, so to speak, unsafe to be unsafe.

You have to choose. You can have patriarchy or not. If not, you will either suffer anarchy—moral, intellectual, and civic—or you will suffer tyranny in your attempt to keep the anarchy from ruining everything, tyranny in the form of the dismal and unproductive safety of the averted eyes and the locked gate. You can have fathers who govern, or else you can have unattached and unaccountable males who take a dismal pleasure in doing nothing or a ferocious pleasure in destroying things—or sometimes alternate between one and then the other. As always, I speak of the general case. But as always, I insist that human institutions and customs must address the general case. Some people are immune to poison ivy, but I wouldn't cut it up for salad. Some people are color-blind, but I do not therefore limit my painting to gray.

No Fathers, No Hope

"The inexpressible sadness which emanates from great cities," says Gabriel Marcel in *Homo Viator* (1952), "a dismal sadness which belongs to everything that is devitalized, everything that represents a self-betrayal of life, appears to me to be bound up in the most intimate fashion with the decay of the family." Marcel wrote those words before the attack on manhood itself—and therefore on fatherhood—was mounted with an unparalleled and unprecedented hatred of nature. Hope is dyed in the soul's grain. Hope is not a mere calculated guess. There is a chasm that separates the husband and wife who treat the child merely as an object of prudence, an heir to succeed them, to be their substitute, from "those who, in a sort of prodigality of their whole being, sow the seed of life without ulterior motive by radiating the life flame which has permeated them and set them aglow." That chasm may as well be as wide as the universe: consider parents who think of the child as a choice, a lifestyle accessory, or a lapdog in a city apartment.

Why do men work, asks the poet Charles Peguy, if not for their children? The father throws himself away in hope, looking forward to the time when he will be no more on earth than a name or a rumor of a name but his children will be alive, and people will say of him—if they remember him at all—that he was a good man but his children are better. He hands on his old tools to his sons, tools shiny with the wear of his hands. He watches his children grow and is proud: he does not want them always to be babies. And when the young children come up to him for a kiss before they go to bed at night, and "they bend their neck laughing like a young, like a beautiful colt, and their neck, and the nape of their neck, and their whole head," the father places his kiss right upon their crown, "the center of their hair, the birth-place, the source, the point of origin of their hair." (This is from *The Portal of the Mystery of Hope*, published posthumously in French in 1929; Peguy himself died a hero's death in 1914, in the first weeks of the Great War.)

Marcel picks up on this insight from Peguy, that fathers are the "great adventurers of the modern world," accepting the risk of a big family, instead of simply "acquiring life as one puts electricity or central heating into a house." The father, he says, makes a creative vow. He does not say, "I will give only so far." I knew a woman once who told her husband that she would agree to have a second child only on condition that he buy her an expensive sports car. He found the arrangement to his taste. That was, as Marcel says, "incompatible with the inward eagerness of a being who is irresistibly impelled to welcome life with gratitude." No one in our time looks askance at a woman living alone with five cats. Our politics and economics seem aimed at producing old women with cats. And whole great sections of society, formal and informal, public and private, look askance at a happily married woman with five children who devotes her day to making a lively home for them. A lonely revolution has it been.

"But the woman, not the man," comes the objection, "must bear the new life within her body, and so it is she and not he who must sacrifice her position at work, and something of her ambitions. You cannot make a father of him without making a mother of her." A strange world, wherein motherhood is considered a sacrifice and not a glory. If you argue that motherhood must be accompanied by physical burdens and pain, and perhaps great disappointment, and the constriction of your freedom, I must ask what you think your work is for. Your joy? Who finds joy in an office? Prestige? How many people in the world will know your name even if you attain the heights of your profession? How many will know it twenty years after you have died? And what is twenty, to the centuries to come? But to bring into the world an immortal soul—another human life, another being that is more beautiful and more complex than all the physical universe besides—that is a trivial thing?

But there is truly an asymmetry between motherhood and fatherhood, and it suggests to us what intellectual, spiritual, and social power is implied in patriarchy. For the father, as Marcel suggests, must make a vow, a promise that the mother does not have to make, and not because he is more important to the child than she is. Quite the reverse. He is far less important, in any immediate physical way. His fatherhood begins in a kind of nothingness, says Marcel. He contributes the seed, and if we were talking about many of the mammals, his work as far as the specific mother and her offspring are concerned would be finished at that point. The female must bear the brood in her body, must suckle it, must clean it, and must tend to it during its time of weakness, until it is grown and can fend for itself.

Human fatherhood is therefore mediated, says Marcel, or rather comes into genuine existence, by means of *a creative vow*. It is akin to the vow that a human being can make to give up his very life. A mother bear may fight a predator to the death to protect her young. That is in her nature. But there is no promise involved; it is pure instinct. The human father, however, has no such overriding instinct. Sometimes he may even look upon the child as an intruder between him and the woman who is the object of his affection. But he makes a promise, a boundlessly creative one. That promise transcends the moment and the place and the tender feelings he may experience as he looks upon the mother and child.

Let me give as an example the account of the birth of Jesus, as we find it in the gospel of Matthew. The Evangelist focuses on Joseph. When he learns that his betrothed, Mary, is with child, and he knows that it is not his own, he considers divorcing her—literally *setting her aside*—because he is a just man, and doing it quietly, because he wishes as little harm as possible to come to Mary. But an angel appears to him in a dream: "Joseph, son of David, do not fear to take Mary your wife, for that which is conceived in her is of the Holy Spirit; she will call his name Jesus"—Hebrew *Yeshua*, meaning *The Lord saves*, "for he will save the people from their sins" (Matthew 1:20–21). We suppose that Joseph is in a most unusual and uncomfortable position, but it is in essential ways the pattern of fatherhood. We fathers are all like Joseph. We cannot know for certain that a child is ours; see Shakespeare's *The Winter's Tale* for the near-tragedy of a father who doubts his fatherhood and in a fit of unjust madness accuses his wife of adultery, to condemn her to death. But beyond that, the father's bond with the child can be tenuous. He must not just accept the child, but also incorporate the child into his creative vow, into his self-devotion for the future—quite aside from any feelings he may or may not have for that child.

We see Joseph do just that. The angel appears to him not simply to tell him of the divine paternity of the child, but to tell him *what he, Joseph, must do* as the child's father here on earth. The medieval artists who with a jocularity in their souls portrayed Joseph at the Nativity as an old man off to the side and sleeping, while Mary gazes lovingly into the eyes of the child, captured a deep and abiding truth. Were we dealing with cats or dogs or other beasts that engage in "casual fruition," to use Milton's words, the sire would not be in the picture at all. But there is Joseph, steeped not in the passion of parental love, but rather in the passion of responsibility. He is dreaming intensely—and learning in those dreams how to protect the mother and child. "Rise," says the angel, when Herod has learned of the new-born king of the Jews, "take the child and his mother, and flee to Egypt, and remain there till I tell you; for Herod is about to search for the child, to destroy him" (Matthew 2:13). Joseph learns in a later dream that it is time to return to Israel, because Herod is dead (2:20). But when he hears that Herod's son is on the throne, he needs no dream to advise him, but clears out of his family's ancestral village of Bethlehem and settles to the north in Galilee, in Nazareth.

We may be tempted to consider these dreams as mere devices to convey the child Jesus from one place to another. But the Evangelist does not consider them so. Even before we hear about the conception or the birth of Jesus, we hear what his place is in a vast history of fatherhood: for this is "the book of the genealogy" (Greek *geneseos*: a new creation, a new *genesis*) "of Jesus Christ, the son of David, the son of Abraham" (Matthew 1:1). We must think of Joseph along with the fathers of old, and this is not just a matter of blood descent. It involves the whole history of a people, as Matthew is careful to point out: "So all the generations from Abraham to David were fourteen generations, and from David to the deportation to Babylon fourteen generations, and from the deportation to Babylon to the Christ fourteen generations" (1:17). Joseph the son of David must protect Jesus, looking forward to what the child will do, and so the promise extends into the distant future, even, as we learn, to the end of time. To Mary is given the much fuller revelation of Jesus and his person and his mission; from Joseph, rather, is required a vow made in a kind of darkness.

Hence patriarchy is a function of hope. Think of the hopelessness of the secular world, which has set its face in stubborn self-destruction against the figure of the father, and ultimately against the fatherhood of God. Where is the hope? No one believes any longer in the saving power of technological progress; we must have fewer people in the world, not more; we demand the so-called right to kill the unborn child, which is feared as a threat, not longed for as a promise; we demand the so-called right to divorce, which is itself a confession that we have nothing to hope for from marriage, but much to dread; we traduce our fathers for not being as wise and as good as we demand, but we dare not call ourselves wise and good in turn, and we do not pause to think of what generations hence will call us. It is not just a gray life without fathers. It is a severely constricted life, bound to the present, not a culture but a mirthless floating along with the suggestions of mass phenomena. Perhaps we may put it this way: be governed by fathers, or let the tiller go, and the ship floats wherever the water takes it. It has no direction: no past, and therefore no future.

Home Is Where the Hands Are

Think of the original juggernaut: an enormous chariot carrying the image of the Hindu goddess Puri. According to the medieval traveler and storyteller John Mandeville, when on the great feast of Puri the chariot is led through the city, pilgrims from far away throng about it, "and some fall down before that chariot and let the wheels go over them, to their death, and some have their arms and shoulders broken to pieces, and they do this out of love for her idol, that they may gain the more joy from it" (*The Travels of John Mandeville*, lines 1652–59). A craze of religious fervor, we may say, and yet how many juggernauts have we tamely permitted to roll over the broken bodies of our families, our local schools, our small businesses, our neighborhoods, our villages and towns, our parishes, our fraternal societies—everything! They were mad with devotion. We are but docile and weak.

The school, run not by your neighbors but by the juggernauts of the teachers' unions, the publishers of textbooks, and the ideologies of the programs that teach the teachers, is not in the business of helping boys to become men and the heads of strong families. Here the edge of what is called "critical theory" turns against those who wield it. Why should the school want to produce strong families? So long as there are families of some sort or another, mostly weak, the school thrives, if you can call it that—I mean that its bulk grows fat and it takes on more and more of the family's tasks and performs them badly enough to warrant calling for more funds. The tapeworm wants a sick dog.

Utopian saviors of the world, such as Karl Marx or his wealthy cad of a friend and financier Friedrich Engels, or such sexual revolutionaries as Wilhelm Reich, despise women but pretend to set them free from man; that supposed liberation is only instrumental to their wish to destroy all that stands in the way of their dreams of total social control. We should commend Marx's poison to his own lips. Who is the tyrant at heart, the cunning money-lender, the driver of slaves? Who but the hater of men's chief strength against the tyrant, the usurer, and the boss? That chief strength dwells in the family and in networks of families.

Hence are teachers trained in arrogance, making so bold as to call themselves "co-parents," reducing father and mother to beggarly clients whose care for their own children is permitted by the state under sufferance. The teachers thus obey the rule of bureaucracy, which is that people rise to the level of their incompetence; their ambition grows in proportion as they abandon, or fail at, the humble but necessary work the parents pay for them to do. I have wondered why President Obama never really used the great goodwill he had from the media to call for a moral revival that would strengthen the family, especially for the poorest among us. But his own parents were antagonistic to the family, and his father played not the patriarch but the irresponsible male; and what advantage could strong families bring to a social system that feeds upon and encourages family dissolution?

Suppose you are an old-fashioned liberal and humanist. You believe that it is *not good* for man to be reduced to masses, subject to machines and their exigencies or to the algorithms of computer programmers that decide what you will see and how you will experience it. The resistance requires strength. Where will you get that strength from? Not from the single mother. She is too hard-pressed. She has not the leisure. Perhaps she has not the inclination, because it is in the woman's nature to be agreeable; woman is more suggestible, as advertisers well know. The man enters the shopping mall to buy a lawn mower, and that is what he does, not bothering with the rest of it, and perhaps he does not buy one at all if the samples look like junk. He may be a little less fussy about the price, but he also tends to buy mainly what he needs, and his needs—his own needs, not the needs of his family—are few. Think of a house in which a man lives alone, and note the bareness of it, a kind of poverty. If you see a small house decked around with flowers, you can be pretty certain that a bachelor does not live there. As always, what is a strength in one sense is a shortcoming in another. More evidence that Saint Paul is right, that man and woman are for each other (see 1 Corinthians 11:8–12).

We will not get persons to stand up against the juggernaut unless we have *families* doing so. And the very people who run the juggernauts testify, grudgingly, that we will not get those families in any appreciable number unless they are headed by fathers, who say, "Thus far and no farther." Let us look at how this is so, in practical terms.

What family on your street can resist the juggernaut of mass-produced food, high in worthless soy that acts like estrogen, high in chemicals that are closer to plastic than to meat and vegetables and fruit, high in engineered gluten that sets the body on the road to diabetes? Not the single mother and her children. They are fortunate if they get a home-cooked meal every day. There is not the leisure, not the time. Not the couple with the two full-time professional jobs; again, there is not the leisure, and probably not the inclination, since such people have been taught to consider their careers as primary and their children as accessories. To grow some of your own food you need a man to do most of the heavy work to prepare a field, and you need a woman devoted to tending the plants and preserving the crop. You have to have a real household *economy*. A healthy and efficient division of labor will develop naturally, and both the man and the woman, to say nothing of the children all brown with a life outdoors, will be stronger and tougher than their fellows who hit the gym once a week to plug themselves into a machine, not to mention those who sink into a couch. There is all the difference in the world—qualitatively, spiritually—between, on the one hand, the merely repetitive action that treats the body as a thing to be kept in good lubrication, like churning the wheel of an upturned bicycle that goes nowhere, while you are listening to canned music or picking heavy weights up only to put them down, and, on the other, tilling, hoeing, weeding, gleaning, milling, canning, and cooking, talking to your children as you do it, or humming or singing a song. People travel far away as tourists to attain to a ginned-up wonder that might be theirs quietly, in the ordinary light of day, if they lived in real families doing real work together.

Let me appeal to a whimsical example. In the summers, my family lives in an old fishing village in Atlantic Canada. Food is everywhere for the gleaning: wild apples that actually taste like apples and not acidulous cardboard; chanterelle mushrooms, impossible to mistake, popping up on a convenient mat of pine needles; clams on the beach; mackerel by the hundreds rushing with the ebbing tide through a narrow channel under a bridge; spruce grouse too stupid to move when you throw rocks their way, let alone aim a gun at them;

choke cherries, and the juicy and intensely sweet saskatoon fruit on trees everywhere, and wild berries—strawberry, raspberry, three varieties of blueberry, gooseberry, blackberry, bilberry, cranberry, and the rich lingonberry—all for the gathering. Yet no one gathers them anymore. I do—and I am always alone doing it. And so at our house we have real pies, and real berries for seasoning, and usually around two hundred jars of jam a year, with much more fruit in them than goes into those jars in the store. My wife and daughter make the jam. It is a delight in many ways—and the food, as I say, is real.

I know many a person on the political left who senses that there is something amiss with the enormous all-purpose markets that sell low-quality goods at low prices and employ people to do the most menial tasks requiring no initiative, no imagination, and no impress of a human mind: products, we may say, without hands. I have some-times jested that the entire economy now depends upon the workers at the fast-food restaurant being *not persons*, but functions. If the cook dared to sprinkle paprika on the hamburger, there would be foreboding signs in the heavens to the westward and a cloud like a man's hand. People who intuit that there is something wrong with our standardized and banalized world are correct, and yet by and large they resist the only feasible solution to the problem. To put it bluntly, you cannot have a world of family businesses without fami-lies, and you cannot have economically productive and socially pow-erful families if they have no order—and that means natural marriage and patriarchy.

You may ask, "But why?" Because it works, that is why, and no other arrangement works nearly as well. The small family business is an excellently human way of doing things, with each member of the family, including the small children, occupied in tasks that benefit the whole. It is a real society in action. For it to succeed, there must be rules and a governor. The wife is the queen of the realm, and the husband is the king. If the wife has more to do with the children when they are still small, and more to do with the intimate features of their common life, the husband will have more to do with the family's foreign policy, as C. S. Lewis puts it in *Mere Christianity*. He is at the city gates. He will be the more likely to set general and long-term aims for the business. But you will see quite clearly that neither the man nor the woman could do without the other, and that interdependence, which is healthy and dynamic for both, makes for gratitude. When labor is mere work to be done regardless of roles or sex, the person who is the more attentive to details—usually the woman—will be frustrated by the person who lets details slide. The person who attends to the form of the whole—usually the man—may think the other person is bogged down in the details. There will be plenty of opportunities for each spouse to think himself or herself put upon, taken advantage of. But if you live with a traditional division of labor, then you cannot get through one day without depending entirely upon your spouse for something that you *do not do*. So you will be more likely to thank God for your spouse and not take that person's gifts for granted. To put it another way: the woman likes to have a roof that does not leak, and the man likes to eat a good meal. They can both hire themselves out for pay as genderless cogs in the machine of the economy and open their financial veins for roofers and carpenters and an endless succession of fast-food meals supplied by strangers who are also cogs in the machine. Or they can rely on each other for the real and ever-treasured things of home, such as good meals prepared with the woman's personal creativity and care for her husband, and a roof mended and tended out of the man's love for his wife and family.

Then there is the education of the children. Again I appeal to every human being, regardless of political persuasion, who senses that there is something deeply wrong, often downright evil, about the current dispensation: cramming hundreds or even several thousand young children in a sprawling school district into buses for two hours a day, adding that sedentary weariness to an already sedentary and wearisome day. I appeal to everyone who sees that such institutions are as unhealthy to the personality as a life inside a box is to the body. I appeal to everyone who understands that standardization presumes mediocrity and produces it, and to everyone who knows a little about how the great geniuses of the past did not have their creative impulses and their restless curiosity stifled but were taught directly by their parents or by a hired tutor at home, or learned by apprenticeship to a master: Michelangelo, Pascal, Bach, Edison, Einstein, Goethe. We hear about the goodness of "diversity," and there is truth in that claim if the word is rightly understood—if the aim is not mere difference for the sake of difference. I agree that the modern world is ever on the brink of a drab monochrome uniformity everywhere, with everyone listening to the same placeless and rootless music, watching the same placeless and rootless shows made for the masses, reading the same few sub-lingual and non-cultural and often mendacious reports in the mass news media, and getting their ideas, such as they are, from advertisers, not from good books or genuine human discussion or experience.

Think of music. The greatest Celtic fiddler in our time may be Natalie MacMaster, who along with her husband Donnell Leahy and their large brood of cheerful and musical children travel about Canada and the United States, playing to big happy crowds. I attended one of their outdoor concerts in Nova Scotia, on the grounds of the country church where they were married. Cousins, families—for this is the music of the fireside, the open field, the farm after the harvest, the shearing of the sheep, not of the academic conservatory, still less of the music industry pasting together sounds of various sorts in the way that a factory stuffs noodle-stuff and vegetable-stuff and broth-stuff into a can of soup, or confects from sugar, mucilage, and titanium dioxide the powder that goes on the torus of gluten that pretends to be a doughnut. What a joy it was to hear real music straight from the hands of a family of human beings, who learned it from their elders and who were passing it along to their children in turn!

Let us then grant that the mass schooling (which is not the same thing at all as universal education) tends to the banal. Grant that it is a bad thing. Many parents now resist it by teaching their children at home. Naturally, most of the responsibility for the education will devolve upon the mother, while the father is working, though by no means do I think it wise to have the father give over that responsibility entirely; he has much to contribute, and he should not be idle about it. But for the home to be that small outpost of intellectual sanity, not a mere place where people feed and sleep and know not one another, there must be order. Much of the mass state's opposition to homeschooling is justified in this sense: homeschooling not only gives the lie to the notion that teachers of children must be drilled and stuffed and pegged by the mass producers of teachers in our colleges; it also shows that long-tested traditional arrangements work. Every such home is its own kingdom, with its laws, its celebrations, its art, its bazaars, and its worship. Every such home is a place where the fiddles may sing.

A Landscape Marked with Castles

Wemmick's house was a little wooden cottage in the midst of plots of garden, and the top of it was cut out and painted like a battery mounted with guns.

"My own doing," said Wemmick. "Looks pretty; don't it?"

That passage is from chapter 25 of *Great Expectations* by Charles Dickens, easily the greatest author in English when it comes to meditating upon economy as the law of the household. In *Great Expectations* he gives us one of his most whimsical illustrations of home *as opposed* to the stringent and often inhuman practices of life among the masses. The clerk Mr. Wemmick, who speaks with implacable severity to the clients of his employer, the London lawyer Mr. Jaggers, has a London self and a Walworth self. In Walworth, where his small home is, he is a gentle and gracious friend. Indeed, he has fitted up his house with a small drawbridge, a flagstaff, and a small cannon, which he fires every evening at nine o'clock Greenwich Time, much to the delight of his elderly and nearly deaf father, whom he calls, with wonderful gamesomeness, the "Aged Parent," or, for short, the "Aged P." Behind the house he has a vegetable garden and a pig, so, he says, "if you can suppose the little place besieged, it would hold out a devil of a time in point of provisions."

"I am my own engineer, and my own carpenter, and my own plumber, and my own gardener, and my own Jack of all Trades," says Wemmick to the young and inexperienced Pip. "Well; it's a good thing, you know. It brushes the Newgate cobwebs away, and pleases the Aged." Newgate is the London prison where Wemmick has to go to communicate with the less fortunate of Jaggers's clients. But Newgate stands in a general way for the entire life of London, as opposed to Walworth.

Wemmick calls his home The Castle, and it really is a castle in the most significant way, over and above the artful little battlements and the moat and bridge. Wemmick has arranged things inside it and has set its governing laws to please himself and the old father he loves dearly. He has also fitted it out to delight his sweetheart Miss Skiffins, whom he will marry, and for whom he has devised the most ingenious little mechanical presents, as she says, "with his own hands out of his own head!"

"A man's home is his castle," goes the proverb, referred to by the jurist Edward Coke in a crucial 1604 case that has helped to determine English and American jurisprudence regarding the right of a homeowner not to be intruded upon, not even, without due warrant, by the executors of government. For, wrote Coke, "The house of every one is to him as his Castle and Fortress as well for defence against injury and violence, as for his repose . . . and the reason of all the same is, because *domus sua cuique est tutissimum refugium*." That Latin dictum translates, "Every man's house is for him a refuge most secure." We do not want to live in a police state. But then we must police ourselves. And the word "man" in the proverb refers to everyone, not only to adult males.

We should consider carefully *why* this principle is correct. Each castle is its own. You cannot have a standardization of castles. The castle is a place of freedom *from*, and freedom *to*: freedom from the leveling tendencies of the mass phenomena, especially mass government, and thus also the freedom to give a wide realm of action to your imagination. Every such castle is a triumph of human diversity.

As always, G. K. Chesterton puts the matter most memorably. "To the moderately poor," he says, and under this heading we may place all people, regardless of wealth, who do not employ servants and who refuse to take their entertainment or their education as given to them by machines, "the home is the only place of liberty. Nay, it is the only place of anarchy. It is the only spot on earth where a man can alter arrangements suddenly, make an experiment or indulge in a whim." Everywhere else is routine, but "for a plain, hard-working man the home is not the one tame place in a world of adventure. It is the one wild place in the world of set rules and set tasks," Chesterton points out in "The Wildness of Domesticity," in

What's Wrong with the World. The question is whether we will take up the challenge, heed the call to be wildly human—to be, as Chesterton says of the husband, "tamed into ferocity" (from "On Household Gods and Goblins," in *The Coloured Lands*). For the wild dog runs, but the watchdog turns and fights.

The Industrial Revolution robbed men of much of their patriarchal influence, by the mere fact that it took them out of the sphere of home and small shop and farm. There have always been soldiers and sailors and traveling merchants, but for the great mass of mankind this separation from the home was new, and not healthy. Often the exhausted, thirsty, and ill-used men would soak their troubles or replenish their lost sweat in beer or hard drink before they staggered home. And if that were not bad enough, the modern world has attempted to right the ship by removing the mother from the home also, rendering it a no-place, a number on a street. Years ago, Hillary Clinton, a woman who must be either remarkably dense or remarkably mendacious, named a book she wrote after an African proverb, since repeated so often that people of good sense are sick of it: "It takes a village to raise a child." But what village? What neighborhood? She wrote to recommend control of children by the furthest thing in the world from a village, namely the vast, impersonal, unfeeling standardized machine of the state. For a woman with the word "village" on her lips, Mrs. Clinton was never to be seen in one; she had fled from Arkansas, a state without a single large city, as fast as she could. It takes mass government or mass industry or both in concert to destroy even the memory of what a village used to be.

The plain fact is that you cannot have a village, or even a neighborhood, unless there are people in that place, dependably, regularly, doing most of their living there, going outdoors, knowing everyone by name and everyone's children also, and that cannot happen without strong and stable families, and you will not have those unless you have fathers committed to the good of their wives and children, providing masculine leadership, governance, and protection. Show me a single healthy, child-rich, self-sustaining, dynamic, culture-preserving and culture-creating village in the world without patriarchs. How long would it take the bigger boys to see that the women cannot catch up with them afoot or in creative mischief? A month or two? Consider a place that is at once far *more patriarchal* and *therefore more matriarchal* than any I have known in the United States. It is the mountaintop village of Tiriolo, Italy, the homestead of my maternal grandfather. It used to swarm with children, but birth control has laid its cold, deadening hand there as elsewhere. But men still take seriously their roles as men, as fathers, and because of that, you may see women and children on the streets at all hours, just being neighbors, talking.

That is precisely why the engineers of the state do not want such families. The state grows by family failure. The ideologies that make for an all-competent state demand family failure and call it freedom. Simone de Beauvoir, writing in *The Second Sex*, said that an enlightened people would make it illegal for a woman to stay at home and take care of her children there. Imagine the fury of hatred behind such a demand. Perhaps she learned it from her cynical and faithless lover, Jean-Paul Sartre. The communist Betty Friedan wanted the same sort of thing. The state is a jealous god, and so are the ideologies that aim their gunsights at the father-headed family. They do not fear that such families will fail. They fear that they will succeed. They are right to fear it. The state wants no castles but its own.

Development?

People will say that my vision of the family is rooted in one form, the American, in one guise, that which prevailed just before the

Sexual Revolution, what I have called the Lonely Revolution. I might call it the Family Moonscape. Just as man was going to the moon, he was rendering his own home barren and bleak.

But I have tried to show the universality of the father-headed family and its absolute necessity for human survival. All right, then. Now that our survival is assured, why, say the critics, must we bind ourselves to the forms of the past, even if they were universal? We no longer walk or ride a horse ten miles to town. We drive a car there and back, and do not suffer for it. Can't we have whatever families we like, we with our wealth and our longevity and our absolute assurance that the human race will continue as long as the earth can bear us?

The first answer is that although the conditions that made us what we are by nature no longer press so hard upon us for our bare survival, still we are what we are—we have the nature we have. The Border Collie does not have to round up sheep. But his inner nature compels him to long to do something like that, and he will not know his fullest joy unless that nature is given its field. Let the secular liberal be consistent. He cannot say in one breath that we are just like the higher apes or other animals, and then in the second breath suggest that we can be whatever we choose to be, like gods detached from the physical world. We do have a human nature. We accept it without question in all matters that are not politically controversial. It is in our nature to need friends. No one doubts that, and no one would say that now we are rich and we live to be eighty years old, we no longer need anybody with whom we may share our joys and sorrows, our thoughts, our hopes, our fears. We would not consider that a "development" of friendship. Cicero defined the friend as someone before whom you may speak your mind aloud as if to yourself. Well, let Cicero have such a friend—as indeed he did, in Atticus. Does anyone say we don't need that anymore? No one talks that way.

Robert Putnam, in his sociological observations of loneliness, *Bowling Alone*, did not say that going by yourself to a largely empty bowling alley was just your working from a new human nature. He viewed it as a sad change in American life. We have always needed friends, and we always will. The same goes for fresh air and good food. And, no less, men and women need what their peculiar sexual natures cry out for, whether or not it is politically correct at the moment, and whether or not they themselves are aware of that need.

Second, even if we concede that it is possible to live without affirming masculinity and femininity, it is quite another to say that we can *live well* without doing so. For the pressure upon man throughout his history on earth has not been bare survival, but *thriving*. And here the false analogy between walking or riding a horse and driving a car to get somewhere begins to reveal something quite different from what the objector intends. The fact is, you really do miss a great deal if you drive that car to town. Your body gets no exercise, so that in order to keep fit, you will have to give it that exercise as it were artificially, by a regimen, a "workout" sadly divorced from play or creative work. You also miss the direct engagement with your surroundings. You miss all the small streams, the grape-hung trees, the birds—once known by everyone, and thus given their common names, such as the yellowhammer and the ovenbird, and now known only by hobbyists. You hardly know your own world. That is a distinct loss. We are willing to accept it, but only as a trade-off, and not as a good thing in itself. And we miss the pace at which we might actually have some real conversations with neighbors. I might note that there is no word for *loneliness* in the English of the Middle Ages, probably because no one experienced it. It is hard to be lonely when you have your family and are constantly around people doing things.

Third, even if we accept the force of the analogy, the objector has drawn the wrong conclusion from it. Man tamed the horse to augment the power of his legs. He wanted to get from Jerusalem to Jericho. Rather than walking, he rode a donkey or a horse. Then man invented the chariot, the horse-drawn carriage, the bicycle, and the automobile. The aim was always more or less the same: to go somewhere. My legs are more powerful than they used to be, at least in this sense: I can get into my car and in a single day travel a distance that would have required two weeks with the best of horses, and months by foot. But what the family has suffered in our times is not like that. No one says that the family headed by a single woman *gets more things done* than the father-headed family got done in the past. The family without a father is, if anything, a receiver of services from without. It is sickly and requires support.

Finally, development implies *unfolding*. When you are a baby, your limbs possess the *potential* to do such things as walk ten miles or climb a tree, but the potential is undeveloped. You can actually do very little. When the cavemen of Lascaux painted the walls with lively scenes of the hunt, their figures were remarkably vivid and interesting—animals in motion! But to say that art had already attained its pinnacle would be absurd. Those cave paintings are great, but they also admit of vast further development. There is much that man the artist had yet to learn about color, and perspective, and the human form and face, and so forth. When you talk about *development*, you do not mean mere *change*. You mean that the developed thing is better than it used to be, more powerful, more alive, more complex and wide-ranging in its action, with more of its faculties in play. The shut bud opens up into all the intricate beauty of the rose.

But is that what has happened to the family? Where, outside of those rare communities where the father-headed family is still overwhelmingly the norm, is the family *the single most powerful political force* in the locality? Where must mayors and school boards and librarians and town councils and local business leaders fear offending against the family, lest they have their heads handed to them? Where are families *the obvious leaders* in local cultural life? If the family has indeed *developed*, what powers does it now possess that were merely latent before? Where is the family big enough and strong enough to be a threat to its enemies? In what town in America are the virtues that make for family life promoted? Do we not rather see the reverse? A society ruled by families might hold parades in which mothers and fathers marched with their children, and divorce, far from being as common as the sale of a house, would be looked on with severe disapproval.

"Where are the Smiths this year?"

"There are no Smiths anymore."

"Shame on them."

Instead we see, celebrated in parade, sexual expression that is unnatural and that does not issue forth in children, as grown men and women in ghastly array and sometimes stark naked advertise their erotic proclivities, and if children are embarrassed, so much the worse for them. Instead we see schools instituting courses and methods of instruction against the wishes of the parents, setting them at defiance; the only good parent is a patsy. Instead we see political bodies rewarding family dissolution, and giving to young boys and girls who want to do the right thing, to marry *before* they have children, not the slightest attention. Inattention? Rather scorn and ridicule. No, the family has not developed. The man coughing up blood has not *developed* a new method of respiration. The amputee has not *developed* a new way to walk. The bedridden old lady who cannot remember your name from one day to the next has not *developed* a new form of social contact. The powers are in abeyance. They are crippled, or dying.

I can say the same thing about marriage that I say about the family. If marriage has *developed*, then we should see it as stronger than ever, more common, more dynamic, more of an influence upon political and cultural life. Marriages should be far *less prone to divorce*, which is just another way of saying that they should be mighty, stalwart enough to overcome the inevitable sorrows and disappointments of our lives. The levee may give way, the locusts may come and devour the harvest, loved ones may die, but the marriage has steel in its backbone and so it endures. Really? Is that what we see? If marriages have *developed*, then they would be more appealing to people, and the clerks handing out licenses would have to sweat every day on account of the long lines. Is that what we see? The movement from a boy whistling to a man playing the violin in a symphony orchestra—that is development. The movement from living in a cave to building a city—that is development. What we are seeing in the case of marriage is not development, but collapse.

And this is in part due, I believe, to ingratitude and confusion. Neither men nor women any longer know what they are to be for one another, so that the attractions between the sexes are reduced to the bare minimum—a pair of breasts here, a muscular torso there. When was the last time you heard a sweet love song about a beautiful woman's eyes? No wonder people have accepted the biologically impossible notion that a man can mate with a man or a woman with a woman. How sad and poor are the imitations of sexual congress, of the act that brings life; how profound a confession of failure. We have forgotten what men and women are, and why they are.

A Human History

But let us suppose that some family arrangement that shoulders the father from his place, or that eliminates him altogether, *could* do those things that it evidently has not done, has no means to do, and shows no promise of doing. Still we must insist that it is not good for man. Why not?

All creatures live in time, but only man has a *history*. The newborn child is not a puppy. He is born into a web of relationships: he is someone's son, someone's brother, someone's cousin. He bears a name. And not just the name by which his mother and father call him. Also the surname, the name of his tribe, his clan. What is it that moves people to search for their distant ancestors? Surely that they feel, without necessarily being able to put it into words, that they are not like jellyfish floating along the waves of time. Man rises above time. He can grasp his existence, he can see it in the context of a family that extends far into the past and will extend far into the future. And it is more than a blood relationship. It is also cultural: there is a sense in which he can say, *We are the Smiths*, and mean to include not only persons but their histories and their way of life.

The father is the key to this transcendence. Think. Forget the slogans, the ideology of sexual indifference, and face what is real. A child's connection with his mother requires no explanation. Body depends upon body. It is the father who requires explanation. The connection with the mother is inward. Think of that archetypal scene of the mother and her infant child. I know of no society's art that focuses upon the father dandling a newborn in his lap. The father has another role to play. It is not accidental that, in culture after culture, the boy is named after his father. He is John Junior, or Andrew son of Simon (Simmons), or Ivan Fyodorovitch, that is, John the son of Theodore. The father orients the child outward, toward the broader society, which is constituted by families that transcend the current age, and which itself has its history. We may say that the connection between mother and child tends to the physical and personal, while the connection between father and child tends to the abstract and cultural. The human person requires both, and urgently.

Let me give the classic myth that brings to light the human triumph over the natural obsession with womb and tomb to produce culture and the rule of law. It is in the *Oresteia*, told by the Greek playwright Aeschylus. The story can be told thus: Agamemnon, king of Mycenae, is leading an army of warriors from all over Greece to vindicate the honor of his brother Menelaus, whose wife Helen has run away with the Trojan prince Paris. Troy is the queen of Asia, across the Aegean Sea. The Greeks' ships are beached at Aulis, and the winds are against them. Agamemnon is told that they will not be able to leave unless he sacrifices his daughter Iphigenia to the chaste hunter-goddess Artemis. He pretends that he wants to give Iphigenia in marriage to his mightiest warrior, the youth Achilles, but when she arrives, she is bound and gagged like a sacrificial heifer—gagged, lest she utter curses against her father. So she meets her death, "to shove his fleet on a bon voyage," as one acid poet would put it four hundred years after Aeschylus. Agamemnon's wife Clytemnestra learns what has happened, and for years and years, while Agamemnon and his hosts are fighting at Troy, she broods and plans revenge.

Agamemnon is not a good man. We need shed no tears for him. When he returns, utterly arrogant and with a female slave in tow, Clytemnestra literally rolls out the red carpet for him, a carpet dyed in the color of royalty, and invites—entices—Agamemnon to tread upon it as he enters his home. He hesitates; he knows what a show of pride it will be. But she persuades him, and that is his last act upon earth. Once he is inside, Clytemnestra tangles him in a net and slays him with her own knife, exulting as she does so. The man has gotten what he deserved. But they have children, the girl Electra and the boy Orestes, and they cannot leave the murder of their father unavenged. Orestes is pressed by the god Apollo to kill Clytemnestra, and when he does so, he is pursued by the Furies, the monstrous underworld divinities that avenge the unnatural act of murdering your blood kin. They are female. Orestes flees then to the protection of the wise goddess Athena, the patroness of Athens, for whose great city-wide religious festival Aeschylus has written his trilogy of plays. Athens, of course, is the city that has invented what we call *democracy*, and Aeschylus's work is partly an investigation into what democracy means, or what it means to be governed by reason rather than by the dark passions of the blood.

We expect that Orestes will be acquitted, though in his trial before a jury of Athenian men, his prosecutors the Furies mainly get the better of his defense attorney Apollo. The jury vote is tied, and Athena breaks the tie by *siding with the father*. When the Furies erupt into wails of agony, crying out that they have been wronged and threatening destruction upon the city, Athena—who had no mother, but was born directly from the head of her father Zeus—makes a bold *political* move. She invites the Furies to be a part of Athenian law and worship. They will be subordinate to the rule of reason, but they will also be given their due. Blood will be honored. When the Furies accept, they become in fact *the Eumenides*, the Kindly Ones. Here is the key: Democracy, which transcends family bonds, is affirmed, but so are the family bonds. The male and the female principles are brought into harmony. The family is not crushed by the new state; rather it is incorporated into it. Athens will no longer be tribe against tribe, clan against clan.

Mothers protect their own. Fathers, in contrast, are responsible for directing their own outward, often at the expense of self-protection, for the common good, so that there may be a city. We cannot say that the family is most powerful where blood ties are everything, because then its domain will be limited. For families to exert mighty influence in the city, there must be a city for them to have an influence in. For families to have a real history, there must be a land of laws wherein the history can take firm root. The families *make the city*, but they make it in part by an act of self-sacrifice. Think of the father who is an umpire at your ballgame. He must not favor his own son, because otherwise there can be no game. But he does favor his own son in a certain sense—by not favoring him, by resisting the appeal of their common blood, by putting the rules above his personal feelings and desires. That makes the game possible. And then the family can excel in the game. Think of the neutral rules—the law—as clearing the field for concerted action.

If you have strong fathers, you can have strong families that have their histories just as the state does, and these families make the state and give it whatever real cultural force it is going to have, but they also resist its encroachments. Think of the dreary barrenness of Soviet culture, in which the family was barely tolerated. Think of the barrenness of our own, now. When I say that I want to support patriarchy, I am saying that I want to live in a real culture, and not in a wasteland. I want the people to govern, the people to build, the people to sing.

CHAPTER FIVE

The Vision

At the end of *La Vita nuova* the young Dante, or rather the narrator of the poem—though at this point it is hard to distinguish them—comes to a momentous decision about Beatrice. She is the girl he first saw and fell in love with when he was nine years old, who then became, in a mysterious way, the great inspiration for his poetry, though their lips and perhaps even their hands never touched. She has passed away, a soul of purity and holiness. But suddenly he has a miraculous vision,

> in which I saw things that made me determine not to write any more about that blessed one, until I might do so in a way more worthy of her. And to attain to it I work as hard as I can, as she truly knows. And so, if it shall please Him by whom all things live, that my life might last for some years yet, I hope to tell of her what has never been told of any woman before. Then may it please Him who is the father of courtesy, that my soul shall travel forth to behold the glory of its lady, that is, the blessed Beatrice, who in

glory gazes upon the face of Him *qui est per omnia saecula benedictus* [who is for all ages blessed].

Ninety percent of wisdom is to notice what is in front of your eyes. Here is something so obvious—literally in the path, so that we might trip over it—that it has become like the song of birds we do not notice, or like the green of the grass and the blue of the sky. The man writes about the woman, placing her at the center of what shall be a grand vision of God, of creation, of human history, of the saga of salvation, and of his own journey from the dark wilderness of sin to the bright fields of heaven. Reverse the sexes, and the whole thing makes no sense. It is not only absurd—as if we were watching dirt-smutched girls playing football while the boys talk about the new dresses at the general store. It feels somehow wrong. No woman has ever written in such a way about a man. We may well ask why not.

I believe there are two main reasons, and they are related. One has to do with vision and the other has to do with love. Let us first consider vision.

What Does It Mean to See?

Let us keep in mind the economy of nature. Men do not see colors with the same boldness that women do. Women do not see things in distant and coordinated motion as keenly as men do. Men often miss the trees for the forest. Women often miss the forest for the trees. We should not be surprised.

Suppose you ask, "Could this breed of mammal survive in the wild if the females ignore their young?" You can hardly get the question out before you see that it is nonsense. Females are for their young. The longer the young are vulnerable, the more sedulous will the female be in their care. They are hers in an immediate and fleshly way, something that cannot be said of the male. It is not controversial to say that a female dog or a female cat is wholly and zealously taken up with the welfare of her puppies and kittens, feeding them from her body, cleaning them, protecting them from threats, warming with the heat of her belly as they sleep. All of her instincts direct her toward these things, which are both a trouble for her and a great and mysterious delight. That it should be so of the females of lower species, but not so of man, whose young are so long in growing and utterly helpless for many years, is simply unbelievable. Every culture testifies to the special bond between mother and child. Go anywhere in the world, and if you are a young woman with a baby or a small child, people will defer to you, and—in healthy societies—women will smile and offer the child a toy or a sweet. Men are not nearly so solicitous for that child.

The woman, in other words, must be—or the human race would not have survived to argue about it—taken up with the child's immediate needs, so that she can move quickly into the most intense focus upon that child. The baby cries; the mother must see what is the matter. In a way that the father cannot really fathom, the child is always a child to the mother. Her tall son with the deep voice and the dark beard on his chin is somehow still the little naked baby squalling and taking his first gulps of cold air in the world. Well have Christians portrayed the Madonna and the Christ Child as an eternal reality, and not just as a passing stage.

Women see deeply into the children they love. What are men looking at, in the meantime? The shiftless man, the man without much masculinity in his spine, may be getting drunk or idling his time away with his buddies, but the manly father is to be found searching the horizon. He sees things in motion. If he misses the intimate details, and if his life is sometimes less warm and bright than his wife's is, he must still see distant things in their mutual relations, and how he and his family fit in them, and what they signify—whether they will protect his family or expose it to danger, whether they present an opportunity or a threat or some of both. This will include, indeed it must include, other families, the whole of the village or city, because a family alone is hardly better than a mountain-man living hand to mouth, catching his prey and skinning it and cramming it into his belly, without seasoning, over a rude fire, with the world around him but a hunting ground and a privy.

So let us consider how men see.

Often it is helpful to look at a phenomenon in its pure and isolated form. I take you to the court of the saintly King Louis IX of France. As the story goes, lords and ladies are gathered around the table for dinner. They talk about the usual things: marriage, horses, silks, new buildings, the latest songs, and so on—that is, they all do except for one portly fellow with the tonsure and the robe of a Dominican friar. When he was a student in Cologne, the mostly German boys called him the Dumb Ox, because the big Italian boy hardly ever said a word, but their master Albert shot back, saying that that ox would someday bellow so loud that all the world would hear him. His name is Thomas, from the castle of Aquino, in southern Italy. He is a cousin of German and Italian royalty, not that he cares about that. The king is fond of him, and often invites him to these dinners.

Suddenly the friar pounds his blacksmith's fist upon the table and cries, "Thus are the Manicheans refuted!"

"Boy," says the king to a page nearby, "go fetch Brother Thomas a pen and paper."

Every man is in some fashion and for some objects and in some ways like Thomas, though he may not be blessed (and cursed) with the same acuity of mind, or blessed (and cursed) with the same drive to systematize, to abstract from the individual, to grasp at the whole.

Imagine Thomas Aquinas taking care of a baby. There is a good chance that the poor thing would fall into the nearest well. That would happen not from carelessness but from the limitations of human vision. We should not expect a Thomas to be a Mary. It would be as if you could be nearsighted and farsighted at once, as if you could focus intensely and simultaneously on both the levels of your bifocal lenses. It's not possible. If you force yourself to try, you will get a headache, and you will probably do poorly at both, rather than well at one or the other. In this regard, a division of labor between the male and the female is expedient, as it is for other purposes also.

We have a tendency to laugh at such men—and it is always men who are this way, not women. I have told my students what a philosopher is: a man who, in a big open field with a single flagpole in the middle of it, will find a way to walk into that flagpole and get a bump on the head. It is easy to imagine Immanuel Kant doing that as he walked about the bridges of Koenigsberg, though to my knowledge he never fell over the side of any. It is easy to imagine Mozart doing it while caught up in a reverie of a hundred strains of sound, though it is said that Mozart could compose in the middle of playing billiards (and there is a deep relation between those two actions). The ancients told the story of the early philosopher Thales, who fell into a ditch because he was looking at the stars. But this same Thales, noticing what other people did not, showed up his critics by paying attention to weather patterns, so that one year he made a killing in the market for olive oil. The great speculators, too, are men, not women. Such men lose their shirts sometimes, but in general they make it possible for there to be any speculations about any goods at all.

Thomas Aquinas was all-involved in love, though not love in the sense of personal and immediate affection for the people around him, whom he may not have even noticed. He was in love with the truth, and that love requires a special kind of vision, a special kind of beholding. Such a man must be oriented toward the *idea* in its underlying Greek sense: not a mere abstraction, but a picture, a thing to be seen. What are such men like? Let us go to Constantinople, and the Council of Nicaea, in 325. The crucial issue will seem trivial, even a distinction without a difference, to people who cannot or will not see its distant implications. The dispute was about whether Christ was *of one being* with the Father—*homo-ousios* in Greek—or whether he was the first created being, not of one being with the Father, but most like unto Him—Greek *homoi-ousios*. In *The Decline and Fall of the Roman Empire*, Edward Gibbon scoffed at the Council of Nicaea, saying that the whole Mediterranean world had to be rocked to its foundations over a diphthong. Yet the odd thing is that Gibbon himself was astute when it came to seeing, and asserting, the larger repercussions of other seemingly minor issues. He was himself a man capable of high levels of abstraction, a system-describer and a system-deviser. It was simply that he did not wish to take the systematic theology of the Christian faith seriously.

The council fathers were not really disputing over vowels. They were disputing about the novel and endlessly fruitful revelation about the life of God that the faith was bringing to the world. "The complex God of the Athanasian Creed," says G. K. Chesterton in *Orthodoxy* (1908),

> may be an enigma to the intellect, but He is far less likely to gather the mystery and cruelty of a Sultan than the lonely god of Omar or Mahomet.... The heart of humanity, especially of European humanity, is certainly much more satisfied by the strange hints and symbols that gather round the Trinitarian idea, the image of a council at which mercy pleads as well as justice, the conception

of a sort of liberty and variety existing even in the inmost chamber of the world.

I do not require that my reader believe that God is one God in three Persons, or that he believe in God at all. The point is to note the masculine habit of insisting on precision on a single detail because upon that small point depends an entire vision of the world—of seeing truths in relation to one another, in a logical or causative hierarchy. To say with Saint John that God is love—not that God happens to love, but that in his inmost being he is love—is to contradict the idea that God is utterly alone in his transcendence, that he is but an impersonal force that animates all the world. Thus had the fathers at Nicaea not insisted upon the co-eternity of the Son with the Father, the faith would long have degenerated into a kindly social club, with some residual reverence for its rather unusual and often embarrassing founder. Instead they affirmed that strange and word-transcending vision of Trinitarian glory.

Consider another, humbler example, which would not attract the watchful care of emperors, abbots, soldiers, and priests. As I have said, men and boys are restless inventors of games, and that kind of invention requires a sort of far-sighted grasp of how the rules, the grounds, the tools, and the human body can interact to make for something fascinating and exciting, or else something dull and predictable. They can always revise a rule book to meet some unforeseen development, but the point is that from the start there is a kind of rule book. And often it is not easy to see why certain rules exist at all, unless you are accustomed to thinking of many disparate items in disparate sorts of motion at once: man, horse, arrow, and deer, or men with sticks, men with arrows, bison, and a direction that leads into a narrow defile where the herd can be cut to pieces.

Take the balk rule in baseball. If a pitcher, with his foot on the pitcher's rubber—for if it is not, he is just one fielder like any other and may do as he pleases—begins to throw to home or to a specific base, but fails to complete the throw in one continuous motion, the ball is declared dead, and every runner advances one base. Even if the feint is unintentional, the umpire will call the balk; even if the ball simply slips out of the pitcher's hand. If you watch a hundred games, you might see the rule called only once or twice. So why is it there at all? To answer that question, you must be able to rearrange a whole set of habits in the game, and ask whether under new governance the result would be better and swifter or more clotted and frustrating. If the pitcher were allowed to fake throws here and there, or to pretend to drop the ball by accident so as to learn on the sly what the runner was planning to do, we might as well have the runners just sit on the bases and do nothing, or the game would degenerate into a back-and-forth between pitcher and runner, while the bat in the batter's hands began to feel like a lead pole, and the fans moaned and threw stale beer onto the field.

Think, then, of constitutions, which men have also devised, as complex machines, games, musical compositions, systems dependent upon men's ability to see interrelations and interactions with as much precision as possible, and upon their understanding that if you change one seemingly small thing you may end up altering the character and the capacity and the action of the whole. Here you need to make a cold appraisal of the passions of men and their desires, and of the dangers of sentimentality. I have heard calls to reduce the voting age in the United States to sixteen. Our founders put it at twenty-one for national elections, and that was in a time when an eighteen-year-old boy would surely have had far more practical experience in the world than our slow-to-grow-up children do now, not to mention a solid knowledge of the classics of Western history and

literature. The argument for lowering the voting age is pure sentiment: It is somehow unfair for intelligent teens to wait to vote. And
should we not hear more from the youth, even from children?

I will not address the matter of maturity, except to say that no
one considers what would be the next move on the chessboard by
whatever dark demon has the misery of mankind as his sole aim.
Childhood would inevitably be sucked into the tornado of political
passion and political bribery, and schools, which should be havens
of leisure for the purpose of learning things that have no immediate
payoff in money or prestige or power, would quickly become snake
pits of enmity and suspicion. There is no way to pave a highway from
the classroom to the Congress and expect that the traffic will all be
in the single direction you want. Most of it will be in the other direction, from those who have the power and the money to those who
do not. And another of the few remaining outposts of humanity, or
at least what might still stand a chance of being human, would be
obliterated. Eliminate the balk rule, and ruin the game.

Or consider a piece of Progressive Era legislation, the Volstead
Act, which made prohibition of alcoholic beverages for personal con-
sumption the law of the land. There was a lot of overlap between the
women who pushed for suffrage and the women at the forefront of
the temperance movement, and it is likely that the women's vote
pushed temperance over the edge. It was a movement steeped in
sentimentality, impelled by feelings that were in some great measure
justified. I have already mentioned the problem it was intended to
solve: Men who spent ten hours a day in filthy, uncomfortable,
back-straining, and dangerous work would be mighty thirsty after-
wards, having lost plenty of weight through sweat, and the most obvious and convivial thing to drink was beer or wine. Drunkenness was
a serious social problem. Wives and children bound to a drunkard
really did suffer. And there were many men, too, who pushed for

temperance. There were the Catholics, the Knights of Father Mathew; I have seen a photograph of a contingent of those Knights marching in an Armistice Day parade in my Irishman-founded hometown, a few days after the most pointless war in modern times came slouching to its end in 1918. Herbert Hoover, a Quaker and a non-combatant hero of the war, called Prohibition a "noble experiment."

Yet it was an innovation with far-reaching consequences. For the first time in the history of the nation, what was essentially a local problem, even a personal problem, was judged to be in the province of the national government. It was as if the king of England should issue a decree regarding bedtime for children. The main problem was not the justice or the wisdom of the act, but its very nature, which tended to grow the national government enormously and to bring all human questions under its purview, so that we can hardly imagine anything—not what goes on in a classroom in South Dakota, not what persons a baker or a florist wants to do business with—about which people will say, "But that is not the business of Washington at all." The complex interlocking actions of different parts of the civic machine were on the way to being replaced by a massive and all-growing and largely unaccountable bureaucracy, acting as a parasite and preserving itself and extending its reach at all costs. Because of the Volstead Act, organized crime went on a grand spree, and so the federal government had to respond with the creation of new agencies. We put Al Capone in prison. But the feds went free. The masculine imperative to set feelings to the side—not to squelch them or to deny their force, but to keep them in their place—and evaluate with a cold eye the practical consequences and the logical implications of the act was overtaken by sentiment, by the call to do something, anything, to help those who were suffering.

You are Dwight Eisenhower, supreme commander of the Allied forces, and you are planning the D-day invasion of Normandy. You know that you will be sending thousands of young men to their deaths. The first to go will suffer the brunt of the counterattacks from German machine guns posted atop the bluffs over the beaches. But somebody must attack, and somebody must go first. There is no avoiding it, unless you want the war to drag on forever, limiting casualties in the short run but perhaps not in the long run, while the enemy, less scrupulous about human life, or more ready to lay down their lives for what they believe, no matter that it is wicked, linger on, waiting you out, knowing that though you may have the material and the tools to defeat them, you have not the will. If the building is burning, sometimes the only way to live is to go straight through the fire. You see it, and you do it. The accusation "You don't care if people suffer" is neither here nor there, as far as the correctness of the strategy is concerned. To say that the man's imperative is to protect his wife and child and, along with other men, to protect and promote the possibilities for a life where women and children will be the center, the heart, is to grant him also the prerogative to determine how that is best to be done, in the long run, in the general case. Otherwise we may win a battle here and there but never a war, and save a finger while the body dies.

So, as I have said and I repeat now, the men of the past should not be despised for not permitting what nobody but a Mary Wollstonecraft or an Elizabeth Cady Stanton here or there even conceived as feasible, let alone desirable, that is, the full participation of women in government. The men should be judged by the general quality of the work they did. And that quality was very high, particularly when you consider that the practical alternative was mere savagery and destitution. I have often told people that I would in a heartbeat renounce my permission to vote in any election, if I could enjoy in return the practical liberty that, for example, a woman in New York enjoyed in 1880. I could keep almost all that I earned, I could teach my children by my own lights without the oversight of the state, I could do business with whomever I pleased and refrain from doing business with whomever I did not please, I could express opinions without coming under the glaring attention of the surveillance state, I could walk for miles in the countryside without fear of molestation, I could walk in the town square at night—and that is not to mention the true liberty that the virtues, most of them stronger then than now, conferred upon the soul, virtues of temperance, prudence, courage, and justice.

Mrs. Van Rensselaer put the matter very well when she said that the moral work of women, the work of educating the hearts and minds of the children in their charge, which was ultimately the work of forming social opinion, was not going to go any better if women abandoned it to take up the executive work of men, and that work would not go better, either, because men would no longer consider themselves, as men, responsible for it. As she warned, the next generation will either be formed, in their moral feelings, by their mothers, or else that maternal charge will be taken up, badly, by the state and mass schooling, mass entertainment, and mass politics. And sure enough, today we stand by as what was once a recognizable culture slumps into incoherence and vulgarity, with the innocence of children betrayed at every pass.

So it is not men who should apologize for what their grandfathers did, but we who must measure what we have done against the record of our grandfathers. The comparison will not be to the credit of the men of the past in every regard, and it is the easiest thing in the world to bring the dead to the bar to accuse them when they cannot defend themselves. But those men of the past built up a civilization where there was none, and they did it with hardly a penny for every dollar we now spend. They did it against the brute resistances and the dangers of the natural world, without our diesel engines, our computer models, our plastics, our synthetic fibers, our labor-saving machines in the home—without the electric light, the refrigerator, the gas stove, and the automobile. Look, just look at any 1900s-era photograph of the town where you live now, and see the sheer variety and vibrancy of public life: a small local school, many small businesses, a playhouse, a music store, a bandstand, a hotel, an ice house, four or five markets, a newspaper, a ballfield, and outside of the imposing edifices of human labor, nothing ugly, and nothing gratuitously loud or shabby or obscene. That was what they built. What have we built now? You will not build, if you do not see. Chartres must be a vision in the soul before it is a cathedral on the plain.

What Do Men Behold?

Feminists have sometimes said that when a man gazes upon a woman, he commits an act of violence. Of course, many a man is a boor and a clod, as many a woman is a harridan and a shrew. But that gaze is a feature of the general human drive to *behold*, and men quite naturally are driven to behold the beauty of women.

I want to draw a distinction between mere seeing and beholding, but before I do so, I should observe that it is perfectly understandable for men and women to look at each other in different ways, simply because what the man needs from the woman is not the same as what the woman needs from the man. She needs his strength, even his aggression. Says Mariana in Shakespeare's *Measure for Measure*, pleading for the life of her husband Angelo, who is morally (though not, as we learn, in actual fact) guilty of rape and murder:

They say, best men are molded out of faults;
And, for the most, become much more the better
For being a little bad; so may my husband. (V.i.441–43)

It should be no surprise that women are attracted to what is dangerous in men, since that danger can be domesticated and trained against the threats to herself and her children, those on two feet or four, or those that come from the lightning, the flood, the pestilence, and fire. Hence a man's scars are handsome to the woman who loves him. Something of that danger attracts Desdemona to Othello. That sweet and sensitive Venetian girl listened as Othello told her father stories of his much-suffering and much-braving past:

> I ran it through, even from my boyish days
> To the very moment that he bade me tell it.
> Wherein I spoke of most disastrous chances,
> Of moving accidents by flood and field,
> Of hairbreadth scapes in the imminent deadly breach,
> Of being taken by the insolent foe
> And sold to slavery, of my redemption thence
> And portance in my travel's history,
> Wherein of antres vast and deserts idle,
> Rough quarries, rocks, and hills whose heads touch heaven,
> It was my hint to speak. Such was my process.
> And of the Cannibals that each other eat,
> The Anthropophagi, and men whose heads
> Grew beneath their shoulders. These things to hear
> Would Desdemona seriously incline. (I.ii.131–45)

That was the "witchcraft" he used on her. It is not a new thing in the world. "I think this tale would win my daughter too," says the Duke of Venice.

What is true of men and women is true of boys and girls. Booth Tarkington's wonderful eleven-year-old boy, Penrod, in the novel by

that name, detests all things female except for the blonde and freck-
led Marjorie Jones. And she is too young to know that she likes him
so much, she just has to insult him: "And but yesterday she had chid
him for his slavish lack of memory in daring to offer her a greeting
on the way to Sunday-school. 'Well! I expect you must forgot I told
you never to speak to me again! If I was a boy, I'd be too proud to
come hanging around people that don't speak to me, even if I WAS
the Worst Boy in Town!'"

Of course she likes Penrod, because, though he is not usually
malicious, he makes things happen, he upsets the dull routine—he
is bold. So she slips him a charmingly misspelled note, the last words
in the novel: "Your my bow."

Men do not look to women for protection. A man looks to a
woman for bounty, tenderness, and patient endurance—she is the
one to be protected, because she will be the one bearing and caring
for his child. Think of the meaning of the most obvious secondary
sex characteristics in the human being. It is not just that the boy's
voice deepens so that it is specially marked for manhood. It is that
the girl's voice *does not deepen*, but remains childlike, "gentle and
low," says King Lear, "an excellent thing in woman" (V.iii.275). It is
not just that the boy's chin and cheek become rough with hair, but
that the woman's chin and cheek do not do so, instead remaining
childlike, and thus they remind the man of the freshness and beauty
and innocence of youth. Creatures with smooth chins and high
voices are to be held immune from violence. So many of our so-called
"double standards" are simply the natural expressions of simple biological aims. We may forgive, in some rather circumscribed social
settings, the sailor who swears like a sailor, because he does the work
of a sailor and fights the elements as a sailor. We find rather unpleasant the daintiness of a man who not only will not wrestle but turns
up his nose at men or boys who do. He is a killjoy. But we find it

understandable if the woman does not care to be nearby as the men sweat and grunt and strain, and we find it unpleasant, even a bit absurd, to hear the skinny-wristed woman with the girl's chin trying to lower her voice into countertenor as she mimics the sailor. It does not work, and it has no point.

So both men and women find women beautiful, because they are: the youthfulness, the gentle curves of the body, and the bell-like voice are powerfully attractive. Milton is not necessarily suggesting anything sinister when his Eve, first awakened at her creation, gazes upon her own beautiful image in a pool of water. There she would have remained forever, she says, except that a voice led her to where Adam was waiting beneath a plane tree—manly indeed, but not so soft, not so winsome as that first watery image. Adam then must pursue her, as she sweetly and generously recalls:

> Thou following criedst aloud, "Return, fair Eve!
> Whom fliest thou? Whom thou fliest, of him thou art,
> His bone, his flesh; to give thee being I lent
> Out of my side to thee, nearest the heart,
> Substantial being, to have thee by my side
> Henceforth an individual solace dear;
> Part of my soul I seek thee, and thee claim
> My other half," with that thy gentle hand
> Seized mine; I yielded, and from that time see
> How beauty is excelled by manly grace,
> And wisdom which alone is truly fair. (4.750–57)

And it is a predictable move when Satan, in the body of a serpent, first addresses Eve and not Adam on that fateful day of temptation and fall. He does not begin by talking about God or deity or knowledge or a tree. He appeals to her sense of her own beauty, "with ravishment beheld," he says, as she is the "fairest image" of her divine Maker. It is no sin for Eve to believe that her beauty is ravishing, since it is, nor that, if the word "fair" is understood aright, she is the fairest creature in the new-made world, since she is. Evil is a parasite, making evil use of the good it cannot of itself create.

Man beholds woman. It is not Eve who gasps with wonder and gratitude at the presence of Adam, but Adam who does so at the presence of Eve: "This at last is bone of my bone and flesh of my flesh" (Genesis 2:23). Who then is superior to whom? The beholder, or she whom he beholds? Who is superior, the young man who braves the cliffs to gather the edelweiss, or the young lady for whom he gathers it, whom he desires to marry? The Swedish boy who fashions and decorates a cedar chest to win the girl he loves, or the girl for whom he does it? Is not the true relation of male and female rather like a dance?

And now let us think about what it means to *behold*. My dog Jasper sees things. His eyes register a grayish range of colors. They detect patterns and motions. So do my eyes, with a better register for color; but eyes do not see things. Only the mind does that. Jasper knows me when he sees me. That he knows me as a human being, I very much doubt, never mind his high intelligence and his obeying eighty commands. He does not think in categories. He does not abstract from his experiences. He looks up and runs to the window when he hears a noise, to see what might be making it. But he does not set out simply to see. It is no accident that words having to do with sight have also to do with the mind: Old English *witan*, to know (see modern English *wit, wise*), is a cousin of the Latin *videre*, to see, and Greek *oida*, I see, and Sanskrit *veda*, to see; the sacred Hindu book called the *Rig Veda* is an ancient collection of hymns and prayers, suggesting that to see, to know the highest things, is to break forth in praise. The Hebrew author of the first chapter of Genesis tells us that as soon as God spoke the light into being, he *saw that it was good*; he is like an artist beholding his work.

To behold is to submit yourself to the beauty of what you behold. It implies a fundamental affirmation, as Josef Pieper says: "How good it is that you exist!" The boy Dante saw Beatrice and was struck with wonder. She would become the object of his wonder, his marvel. "O you wonder!" cries Ferdinand when he sees the noble Miranda for the first time; she, with a great capacity for wonder, as on her desert island she has never seen another human being besides herself and the hag-seed Caliban, has already said of Ferdinand,

> I might call him
> A thing divine; for nothing natural
> I ever saw so noble. (*The Tempest*, I.ii.420–22)

But mainly it is man who beholds woman. Here is Edmund Spenser, describing the power that the eyes of his beloved exert upon him:

> More than most fair, full of the living Fire,
> Kindled above, unto the Maker near:
> No Eyes, but Joys, in which all Powers conspire,
> That to the World nought else be counted dear;
> Through your bright Beams doth not the blinded Guest
> Shoot out his Darts to base Affection's Wound,
> But Angels come to lead frail Minds to rest
> In chaste Desires, on heavenly Beauty bound.
> You frame my Thoughts, and fashion me within;
> You stop my Tongue, and reach my Heart to speak;
> You calm the Storm that Passion did begin,
> Strong through your Cause, but by your Virtue weak.

Dark is the World, where your light shined never;
Well is he born, that may behold you ever.
(*Amoretti*, sonnet 8)

What we notice here is that the eyes of the woman direct the lover's eyes not simply to her, and certainly not to mere "base affection," but to God, the Maker himself. Her virtue "calm[s] the storm that passion did begin," leading him forward on the journey to heavenly beauty. To behold her eyes is to be blessed, as if one were looking upon the face of God. Lest anyone say, "There is another thing he wishes to enjoy with the woman," Spenser cheerfully agrees. This is how he describes his merry impatience on his wedding day, which fell on the summer solstice, the longest day of the year:

Ah, when will this long weary day have end,
And lend me leave to come unto my love!

If we can no longer appreciate how a man can, at one and the same time, be enthralled by the heavenly beauty of a woman's eyes, and want to do with her, in marriage, the child-making thing, that is itself a symptom of our poverty of soul.

Suppose we grant what appears to be the case in every culture, that women adorn themselves to attract the gaze of the men, and that the men, at their best and holiest, do not simply gawk at them but *behold* them, and admire them. Is this something for which men must apologize? I think of Camille Pissarro's 1892 painting, *The Poultry Market*. It is thronged by cheerful peasant women who have come to the market to buy and sell, but the main figures in the foreground dominate the scene. One is an old man, sitting on a bench, looking at the other, a comely young woman, dressed handsomely, carrying a basket in one hand, while her other hand rests on her hip. Her eyes are cast down, as might naturally be the case if your business is done and you are going home. She may well be with child. The gaze of the old man seems calm and appreciative. Nothing is wrong. He sees her beauty, and without saying so, he declares that it is good. To call him a "dirty old man" is to betray a dirty mind. If beauty is not for beholding, what is?

A Farther Vision

As I have suggested of other features and faculties for which men are noted, this impulse to behold the woman does not simply rest inert when women are not around. To call it a drive to "objectify" them misses the point entirely, since the beholder is in the most fundamental way dependent upon what he beholds. In a sense he is "objectifying" himself, saying *I am a mere object in comparison with what I am looking on.*

Let us go back more than two thousand years. An old man and a youth, sitting by a rushing stream on a road just outside of the city, are talking about love and beauty. The young man, Phaedrus, has been reciting from memory an oration that a grown man has addressed to him, basically to seduce him. It is a piece of cynicism. You should give yourself to me, says the seducer, *because I do not love you.* The typical lover, says this cunning seducer, is given to false-hood, and "commends anything you say or do even when it is amiss, partly from fear that he may offend you, partly because his passion impairs his own judgment" (Plato, *Phaedrus*, 233a).[1] But I will not be that way, "for I am the master of myself, rather than the victim of love," and so I can best work for our mutual advantage (233c, 234c).

This seducer is quite bold: he does not see beauty, and he does not wish to see it. He sees a finely fashioned body, perhaps, but that is all. Were he among us now, he would go trawling for strange flesh on the internet. The old man, Socrates, gently warns Phaedrus against such a pursuer, and instructs him instead on a "madness that is heaven-sent," a madness that issues forth in prophecy and poetry and love (244a–b). We are to imagine the human soul as a charioteer with a pair of winged horses, one of them good and noble, the other wayward. If we were just like the immortal gods, says Socrates, we would climb easily with a pair of good horses and attain the summit of the world, behold the heavens and the earth in their eternal order, and discern justice, which is the very self of the soul, and "likewise temperance, and knowledge," not just the shifting knowledge of things that pass away, "but the veritable knowledge of being that veritably is" (247d–e). Because the soul is nourished by contemplation. Even we, troubled as we are with the wayward horse that represents our fleshly appetites, strive to attain the vision the gods enjoy, and love is our motive force, love that is stirred by beauty, which "was ours to see in all its brightness in those days when, amidst that happy company, we beheld with our eyes that blessed vision, ourselves in the train of Zeus, others following some other god; then were we all initiated into that mystery which is rightly accounted blessed beyond all others; whole and unblemished were we that did celebrate it, untouched by the evils that awaited us in days to come" (250b–c). Even in our current imperfect circumstances, the noblest men still fall in love with an apprehension of the truth and long to see it and to drink from its beauty. To say that such things as truth, beauty, and goodness are mere cultural preferences or meaningless words is to counsel blindness and despair. No wonder there is no Dante in our midst.

As always, we must speak in general terms, because man and woman are more alike than unlike, and though they may strive to reach the true home of the soul by separate ways, yet the home is ultimately the same. Still we can note differences. When the great

women saints and mystics speak of God, he is the passionate one who
pursues them, who invites them into a personal relationship. He is
the lover. And of course it is not wrong to experience him in this
way. This is precisely what a nameless priest once recommended to
the women in his charge, anchorites, each living alone in her cell.
The Rule for Anchorites begs the women to imagine Jesus as a wooer
of their souls who says to them, "Your love—it is either to give, or
to sell, or to be ravished and taken by main force. If it is to give,
where can you bestow it better than upon me? Am I not the most
beautiful of all things? Am I not the richest king? Am I not kin to
the highest? Am I not the wisest of men? Am I not the most courtly?
Am I not the freest to give good things? For people will say of a generous man who can hold nothing back that he has his hands
pierced—as mine are. Am I not of all things the most fragrant and
the sweetest?" (folio 107, verso).

"Stab me in the heart, Jesus," cries the fat wife of the hired man
in Flannery O'Connor's story "Greenleaf," as she takes newspaper
clippings of disasters and plagues and murders and spreads them on
the ground in the woods, flopping down upon them and flailing and
moaning like a fabulous beast in the paroxysms of sexual heat.[2] Or
we may think of that good woman Margery Kempe, whose husband
surely must have been spared any tick of the clock in purgatory,
attending Mass on Good Friday:

> The memory of our Lady's sorrows, which she suffered
> when she beheld his precious body hanging on the cross
> and then buried before her eyes, suddenly filled the heart
> of this creature. Her mind was drawn wholly into the
> Passion of our Lord Jesus Christ, whom she beheld with
> her spiritual eye in the sight of her soul as truly as if she
> had seen his precious body beaten, scourged and

crucified with her bodily eye, which sight and spiritual beholding worked by grace so fervently in her mind, wounding her with pity and compassion, so that she sobbed, roared and cried, "I die, I die," so that many people were astonished at her, and wondered what was the matter with her. And the more she tried to keep herself from crying, the louder she cried, for it was not in her power to take it or leave it, but as God would send it. . . . And this manner of crying lasted for a period of ten years. (*The Book of Margery Kempe*, chapter 57 [1521])[3]

Men are—not like that. Consider it both a shortcoming and a strength, or perhaps an inclination toward a different kind of strength, a different faculty and power.

Here is Dante again, in the opening lines of the *Paradise*:

The glory of the One who moves all things
penetrates the universe with light,
more radiant in one part and elsewhere less;
I have been in that heaven he makes most bright,
and seen things neither mind can hold nor tongue
utter, when one descends from such great height,
For as we near the One for whom we long,
our intellects so plunge into the deep,
memory cannot follow where we go.
Nevertheless what small part I can keep
of that holy kingdom treasured in my heart
will now become the matter of my song. (1.1–12)

If the woman's tendency is to draw all things inward toward the most intimate reaches of the soul, to dwell in the inmost cells of Teresa of Avila's interior castle, it seems that the man's tendency is to broaden out, to spread the vistas wide. The feminine tendency is toward the immanent, the personal; and its danger is emotionalism. The masculine tendency is toward the transcendent, the beyond-personal; and its danger is abstraction.

But if we have to order the two tendencies, the one that should govern the other is the transcendent; it is the leader. The risk in seeing the divine as immanent in all things is that we may lose ourselves in the things and call divine what is just a powerful feeling. Thus we must rise to a vision of the divine. The great male mystics, such as Plotinus, strike us at first as cold and distant. But how can we most closely approach the divine? By a clean and clear subordination of our passions, which spring at least in part from what is irrational in us, to our reason:

> There will be no battling in the Soul: the mere intervention of Reason is enough: the lower nature will stand in such awe of Reason that for any slightest movement it has made it will grieve, and censure its own weakness, in not having kept low and still in the presence of its lord.
>
> In all this there is no sin—there is only matter of discipline—but our concern is not merely to be sinless but to be God.
>
> As long as there is any such involuntary action, the nature is twofold, God and Demi-God, or rather God in association with a nature of a lower power: when all the involuntary is suppressed, there is God unmingled, a Divine Being of those that follow upon The First.
>
> For, at this height, the man is the very being that came from the Supreme. The primal excellence restored, the essential man is There: entering this sphere, he has associated

himself with the reasoning phase of his nature and this he will lead up into likeness with his highest self, as far as earthly mind is capable, so that if possible it shall never be inclined to, and at the least never adopt, any course displeasing to its overlord. (*The Enneads*, 1.5–6)[4]

Such a soul contemplates "all that exists, in the Intellectual Principle." Or, as the sage Lao-Tzu says, "Man takes his law from the Earth; the Earth takes its law from Heaven; Heaven takes its law from the Tao. The law of the Tao is its being what it is."[5] To follow the Tao is to become most real by renouncing what the world takes as most personal and most important. Or, in these words of the unknown Syrian monk who called himself by the name of Dionysius, the Athenian convert of Saint Paul, those souls that have imitated as far as possible the condition of the angels, uniting themselves thus with the divine, "discover that although it is the cause of everything, it is not a thing since it transcends all things in a manner beyond being." To be a "lover of the truth which is above all truth" is to know that no word is adequate to describe it, but also that it is the cause of all things, and that all things are in love with it in their proper ways; "the intelligent and rational long for it by way of knowledge" (*The Divine Names*, 593c d).[6]

Men climb mountains to see.

Man thus is the great maker of *theories*. In their lowest form, these are intellectual games. Every game is characterized by rules and restrictive conditions. The pawns can move forward only, but they capture only diagonally. Very often, the restrictive conditions are necessary if you are going to make any headway in a particular branch of knowledge. It is not simply the case that Darwin devised his theory of evolution from what he saw, but that the theory of evolution enabled him to see things that he may or may not have been looking for. Consider his theory as a game whose prime rule is that no change in a creature's structure may come about except by random chance. Other theories are games on other lawns, with other rules. The game of Marxism has its own prime rule, which is that all human phenomena must be resolved into an economic and political motive. Marx did not simply derive this game from his observations; the theory allowed him to see things that he otherwise would have missed. Of course, your theory may be wrong—and then you see things that are not there, you attribute false causes or motives, or you miss things that are there. Marx was cursed with a dogged industriousness and relentless logic, so he went far wrong indeed. A woman would have been called up short by having to cook dinner.

Other theories will not do violence to the material world and to human actions in it, because they are not about that world; they are theories in the mind-created world of the theoretic game itself. What made the young Carl Friedrich Gauss bend the great might of his intellect to discover how to construct a regular heptadecagon (seventeen sides) with only a compass and a straightedge? If we want only the pragmatic, there is no point to such an enterprise. We can more easily measure out the circumference of a circle, divide it by seventeen, and use a marked string to find the points we need for the vertices. And why would we want such a thing at all? But the drive for conquest is a drive for seeing truths that lie hidden. If you can do it for a figure with seventeen sides, can you do it for a figure with only seven? No, you can't. Then for which numbers, and why? Gauss kept on, and showed an unexpected connection between this portion of geometry and an apparently unrelated portion of number theory dealing with prime numbers of a certain kind, the so-called Fermat primes. All kinds of practical consequences have flowed, distantly, from the discoveries of theoretical pioneers, who were in love with truth within the bounds of their most beloved theoretical inventions and games. Were it not for investigations into prime numbers, reader, much of what we do to keep computer information secure would be impossible.

But the motive for Gauss was the beauty of what he sought. It is like climbing a mountain. Down below, all is a tangle of paths and hills and rocks and streams and woods; above, things assume their place in a single comprehensive view. It is breathtaking. You toss a ball into the air. How fast is it traveling at any given point in time? We know that it speeds up the farther it falls, but how and how much? If you are Isaac Newton and you want to answer that question, you will have to invent an idea—again, a picture in the mind—of something that had hitherto not been conceived: an idea of the sum of numbers infinitesimally small. So you invent calculus. Archimedes had come within a whisker of inventing it two thousand years before, and had he done so there is no telling what the history of the world would have been—his motive would have been nothing but the beauty of the truth. The apocryphal legend about the apple plunking Newton on the head is more revealing than we may suppose. It implies a man strangely set apart from the immediate needs of the body, apart from social bonds; he is free to ask whether a planet may be like that apple in its motion. How does the answer to that question put bread on the table? Not immediately or directly. Yet in answering that question, Newton more than any man may be called the creator of the modern world, with its amazing advances in technology which have put bread on billions of tables.

At its noblest, though, theory is for seeing all that is true. It seems strangely dispassionate to most of us, but not to the people who strive for it with all their heart and soul; it is beyond the passions of the day, because its passion is for eternity. The Greek word *theoria* suggests a spectator looking upon the stage: he has a *thea*, a view. The word is a cousin to *thauma*, a wonder. The Latin *mirus* describes something

to behold as a marvel, especially something delightful: so we find that
it is a distant cousin to English *smile*. Our very word *wonder* comes
from an ancient root that signifies what stirs the soul with desire,
with love, and thus it is a cousin of Latin *Venus*, the goddess of love
and beauty. Dante captures perfectly the delight that proceeds from
theory in this sense:

> "To Father and to Son and Holy Ghost,"
> sang all the heavens, "glory!"—filling me
> with drunken joy; it seemed what I beheld
> Was laughter of the universe, the glee
> of laughter whose inebriating swell
> enters by what you hear and what you see.
> (*Paradise*, 27.1–6)

Perhaps we may say that men and women go blessedly mad in
different ways. It is near impossible to imagine a man as Margery
Kempe, weeping so loudly at the Good Friday service that a priest
had to lift her up and carry her away. It is also near impossible to
imagine a woman as Benjamin Franklin, out in the middle of a storm
with a kite and a metal key, risking being struck by lightning and
electrocuted. Why did he do that? Why did Louis Agassiz have himself lowered on a rope hundreds of feet into the depths of a glacial
crevasse? What was John Muir doing on the spur of a glacier on a
foggy day, when one false step could mean instant death? Why did
Henry Hudson sail his ship into that interminable bay that now bears
his name, where his mutinous men either slew him and threw his
body into the deep or marooned him on a treeless island? In one way
or another, they all wanted to *see*. You do none of these mad things
unless your soul is thrilled with a desire to see, to know—not par-
ticulars, but the great vast scene.

The beloved disciple John was perhaps closer to Jesus than any of the apostles, closer even than Peter, whom Jesus called the Rock upon which he would build his church. But he does not describe what color hair Jesus had, or how he walked, or what he liked to eat for lunch. No doubt he knew those things; in fact he implies that he knew them. But it is with the soul of a beholder, of a Georg Cantor considering kinds of infinity, of Michelangelo gazing upon the human person as made in the image of God, of the young Dante seeing in Beatrice the intimations of all that is blessed, that he writes these words:

> That which was from the beginning, which we have heard, which we have seen with our own eyes, which we have looked upon, and our hands have handled, of the Word of life;
>
> (For the life was manifested, and we have seen it, and bear witness, and show unto you that eternal life, which was with the Father, and was manifested unto us;)
>
> That which we have seen and heard declare we unto you, that ye also may have fellowship with us; and truly our fellowship is with the Father, and with his Son Jesus Christ. (1 John 1:1–3)

Our secular physicists may not enjoy being mentioned as in the same category as John (though subordinate in station). But that is an accident of cultural history. In a saner and wiser world, they would gaze together with him, and fall to their knees in wonder.

CHAPTER SIX

The Father in Heaven

I have discussed Jesus' choice to bring twelve men together from different walks of life to be his apostles, and why that choice was both a natural expression of the masculine drive for brotherhood and the most effectual choice, since such men become members of a team, and the team is more than the sum of its members. Such teams have built the world, and not ultimately for themselves, but for families—for the women and the children who are at the center of those families.

There is more to that brotherhood of the apostles, though. Again we must bring into play all that we observe about the man, about the whole mind-and-body makeup of the creature. Let us repeat: The man is physically stronger than the woman. Barring old age or some debilitating defect or illness, and assuming that both men and women will be doing physical work, much of it outdoors, there will for all practical purposes be no overlap between the sexes. The weakest man, if he is at all physically fit, will be stronger than the strongest woman. And remember, cultures work by the norm and not by the exception.

And men's physical strength is united to a spirit that seeks action—the arrow of agency. The two go together. You see a road that winds for thirty miles to get around a mountain, and you say, "Let's blast a hole *through it.*" You see a handsome block of stone and you say, "Give me hammers and chisels and rasps and files, and let me make something out of that rock." You learn of the conjecture that every even integer is the sum of two prime numbers, and you say, "I am going to wrestle those numbers to the ground." I am not just talking about a desire to vanquish. You have to have fallen in a kind of love with the prime numbers to want to do that.

And that passion, strange and productive, is distantly analogous to man's love for woman. Why do men call the ship they love by the feminine pronoun "she"? The invidious way to look at it is to say that the men are reducing women to objects, like ships. But the more revealing and fruitful way to look at it is that the men are elevating the objects to a kind of personhood. Such pronouns are usually employed with affection or admiration. "Thar she blows!" cries the whaler when the leviathan of the deep comes to the surface to spout. The "she" may demand from the man his utmost, and the good man is willing to respond accordingly.

But men will not generally get great things done as loners. There is no such thing as an army of one. Therefore they must unite and form the brotherhood, the team. The phenomenon is universal to human cultures. The desire for agency must remain mostly inert unless the men unite, and they do so not by way of addition, generally, but by the creation of a new thing, one that coordinates specific simultaneous actions towards a common goal. This new thing must, to be most effectual, be organized, which is to say it must possess the features of an organism, and those are hierarchical. The foot is not the head. But within this hierarchy we find equality also: the foot is no less a member of the body than the head is. Every member is for every other, and all together are for the thriving of the organism. That is what Saint Paul is talking about when he urges the fractious brethren of the church at Corinth to cease their bickering. He does not say that every member is equal. The Greeks, with their long history of democratic institutions, would have found that rather easy to understand. What they would have found harder to understand is how in Christianity equality and freedom are compatible with obedience and hierarchy: the man who is the director in one respect must be subordinate in another. Even Milton's devils understand the point, "for orders and degrees," says Satan—correctly—"Jar not with liberty, but well consist."

The cast of mind that makes the team makes also other organism-like things, such as machines and the complex games of formal education, law, and government. The boy invents baseball, and the man invents the separation of national powers and their interlocking functions, with hierarchy built into their equality. The boy turns a doll, a plank of wood, and three cinder blocks into a catapult—I have seen it with my own eyes, and gone over to help it along. The man turns a crew of slouch-shouldered young recruits into a fighting force.

But why bother to have armies, or a tunnel through a mountain, or a ship on the sea, when you can take your ease and live hand to mouth? Only for the family does man in general do such things; only for his wife and children, either those he has or those he hopes someday to have, or, most selflessly, for the wives and children of the community generally. Or perhaps I should put it this way. The men hanging like daredevils from the ropes slung two hundred feet high around the spire of a new cathedral are not thinking, "I am doing this for my wife." But were it not for the family, they would not do it. The loves are integrated. It is not a mere job for them. It is a fulfillment of their fatherhood and their brotherhood at once.

And now we may leap from the brutely practical to the good that transcends the needs of the day; from what is good because we can use it, to what is good in itself to behold and cherish. I have said that men are great beholders. Unless they were so, I doubt very much that we could have gotten from them any of the practical devices, animate or inanimate, that we take for granted. Men seek not to be regarded as beautiful, but to regard beauty: the direction of their vision is less inward and personal than outward, to grow the greater by basking in the light of what transcends their person. Feminists who say that "the personal is the political" do an injustice to both realms. While persons are the moving parts in the game of politics, politics cannot work—any more than any other machine or game; think of the umpire in baseball—unless the strictly personal is set aside or transcended. And the personal cannot thrive, cannot be its beautiful self, if it is forced into the levers and pulleys of the political game.

So it makes sense that women are the prime movers of the child's moral imagination—an intensely personal thing, as is right and just—and men are the prime movers of the theological imagination. I am speaking here in broadly general terms, but I believe they are accurate. The great Christian icon of woman's engagement with the divine is Mary, receiving the Word of God into her heart and her womb. The great Christian icons of man's engagement with the divine—none of them as powerful as the image of Mary—are confrontational, fraught with danger and wonder. Think of Abraham on Mount Moriah, ready to sacrifice his beloved son Isaac, or Moses before the mysterious burning bush, or Isaiah crying out, "Woe is me! For I am lost; for I am a man with unclean lips, and I dwell in the midst of a people of unclean lips; for my eyes have seen the King, the Lord of hosts!" (Isaiah 6:5). Think of the Transfiguration of Christ, with Peter "not knowing what he said" (Luke 9:33), crying out to Jesus that they should set up some booths for Jesus and Moses and Elijah.

Many a man goes to God for comfort. That is a good and proper thing. But he is more likely to go to God first to behold his glory and power. And on the quest for that vision, he turns naturally to the man of God to lead him. He fears that his mother will tell him what he wants to hear or what she wants to hear. He has some hope that his father will instead tell him what he does not want to hear. Or he does want it—but life would be easier if it were not true.

The Elder Speaks

"Lord, teach us to pray, as John taught his disciples," says one of the disciples to Jesus (Luke 11:1). Let us think about this.

First, there are *disciples*. We are too accustomed to the word perhaps to notice its implications of hierarchy. They are, literally, *pupils*—Greek *mathetai*, like boys learning the alphabet. I am fond of the Anglo-Saxon rendering, *leornungcnihtas*, "learning-knights," that is, servants whose job it is to learn from the master. Again, they do not give up their manhood by the subordination. They gain a powerful expression of it. The big fellow whose strength lies idle becomes a linebacker on the football team, and if the coach says he must be in bed before nine at night, he obeys. In fact, in his old age he will boast of his coach's severity, so long as that severity was life-enhancing, with an aim.

Second, the disciple takes the whole arrangement for granted. John the Baptist had his disciples. That is what a man of God has. And the most important thing the man of God does for his followers is to teach them how to pray, that is, how to enter by word and deed into a right and subordinate relationship to God. This *how* is crucial. If you are a Roman priest and the commander of the army wants an omen for how the battle tomorrow may go, you must be skilled in the exact words to say (many of them obsolete) and the exact motions to make, in the precise order, to get the thing done. You fetch the sacrificial animal, you slay it, and you examine its entrails. The Romans were a sophisticated people, but in this regard they were like those tribes of American natives whose medicine men also required skill in precise chants and dances. The boy goes to the man and asks, "How do you accomplish this?" And the priest brings out the snakeskin.

But the third thing, lying in open sight, is that neither John nor Jesus nor their disciples were about exactness in ceremony so as to force the divine hand. That is not the Jewish faith at all, and it is not the Christian faith. The psalmist says, "Your face, Lord, do I seek" (Psalm 27:8). "Beloved," says Saint John to his disciples, "we are God's children now; it does not yet appear what we shall be, but we know that when he appears we shall be like him, for we shall see him as he is" (1 John 3:2). When the disciples ask Jesus how they should pray, they are asking him to help them seek the face of God. They are asking the man of vision to open up the vision to them.

And this again is in perfect concord with man's nature. There are heroes in war. There are heroes in vision. Think of the youth Alyosha in Dostoyevsky's *The Brothers Karamazov*, faithfully following the Elder Father Zossima, whom he loves dearly, and upon whose every word he hangs, intent. We do not wonder at the group of priests and young men who gather about the aged and dying priest to hear his last words of advice and consolation. We assume that it is perfectly natural for them to do so. Alyosha, clear of vision and pure in heart, will in turn become the center of a ring of hero-honoring boys; that group of boys has their own natural leader, Kolya. "Hurrah for Karamazov!" are the last words in the novel—the words of a band of brothers, cheering the elder among them, not because he is powerfully built and bosses people around, but *because he sees things*, and the boys wish also to see and not be stupid forever.

I will hardly stand alone when I suggest that women are not generally interested in encouraging boys and men to press their minds to the utmost, to set all things on the table, daring to lose them all in the search for truth. The feminists themselves confess it, unwittingly, in a variety of ways. The very existence of women's studies programs—those softball fields of the intellect—testifies to it. I am not speaking here about single-sex education, or single-sex groups, which I believe are good things in themselves. The women of a village who gather together at a market to sell their wares are enjoying themselves, confirming their bonds of friendship, giving their children a grand time in the open air, and doing what redounds to the good of their households. The men in the work team are likewise contributing as men to the common good, and the sometime separation of the sexes makes their coming together again all the sweeter. But the women's studies program is not like that. It is predicated upon a falsehood: that the interests of men and women are severable. The idea is not to gather together as women so that when you meet the menfolk again you can have a merry dance and a feast. It is to *retire from men* in a touchy resentment, to keep them away, not because you want to build strong friendships among yourselves for the ultimate good of the men you love, but because you want to keep the love of man and woman from flourishing. Imagine a coffee klatsch of embittered divorcees, their finger-ends yellow with nicotine, gathering the young women about them to magnify the bad things their former husbands did, while smiling cynically should any young lady profess to be attracted to a boy who appears to be wholesome, generous, and manly.

No, the last thing the women in such programs want around are all-inquisitive and all-challenging young men who will press them, saying, "How do you know that? What is the evidence? What does man's history have to say about it?" I am sure that many of my readers will be able to supply their own stories of brave feminist teachers and professors who, as soon as they were put to the test, slapped the Damsel in Distress card on the table and went wailing to the authorities, to the Big Daddy of a bureaucracy, to punish the aggressive and offensive boy. Or they played the Hell Hath No Fury card, not taking the challenge in the spirit of dynamic enmity, as steel sharpens steel, but as a personal affront to be avenged. The boy with the rough chin and the growl in the voice is under the thumb of the woman teacher, and feels uncomfortable there, as she feels uncomfortable as he stands before her. Of course, this is not always the case. But we are speaking about a general and quite powerful reality. I do not say that women cannot teach boys, but that boys will need some men to teach them and may just follow one or two such men to the limits of human understanding. And I say that such women as we in our feminist time have produced *have failed mightily* at teaching boys and men, and seem quite content to have failed, just as the female pastors do not worry overmuch when the young men fade away from their denominations. Such a trouble it is to keep men in line.

We are at liberty to pretend that men and boys are not what they are. We are at liberty to do a lot of foolish things, and to pay for the folly. We may step out of the window of a twenty-story building, believing ourselves to be supermen. Do not blame gravity if it declines to play along. Those schoolboys in *The Brothers Karamazov* were not going to follow an older girl. Neither they nor she would expect it, and not because the boys were conservative—indeed, their leader thinks of himself as quite the progressive and free-thinking sort. It is because she does not represent the general of the army, the chief of the hunting party, the man who has blazed a trail of thought and cleared a path up the mountain. What woman actually desires to be such a captain for boys and men? When a woman says, "I want to be a priest," she does not mean, "I want to lead an army to take the secular world by the throat, and since I know that that will not happen without the dynamism of men, I will lead them to victory." Indeed, female preachers in many a mainline protestant denomination seem content with the aging and shriveling up of their churches. There is no urgency, because the faith has been reduced to kindness and following along with the latest socially approved attitudes. What difference does it make to a mother-god—or to the Christian God reduced to a divine eunuch—whether John and Mary get married before they live together and have children, or whether John and Harry do with their bodies what human bodies were not made to do? The female priest is there to provide comfort and good feeling.

So men go to the elder, the one who is wise—the very word "wisdom" has to do with sight. The disciples are asking Jesus to help them to see.

Jesus replies by giving us what we call the Lord's Prayer. We are apt to take the words for granted, because we have heard them too often. Its first words are, "Our Father." That would have been a single word in Aramaic, with a suffix for the possessive pronoun; if Jesus spoke the prayer in the sacred language of his people, Hebrew, he would have said, *Abenu b'shamayim*, two words, for "Our Father who art in heaven." The structure of the prayer is that of a Hebrew poem: Jesus wants his disciples to be able to commit it to memory. It is powerfully terse and precisely organized. But why *Father*, and not *Mother*, or the more impersonal *Parent*?

Before I address that question, I would like to bring up a powerfully suggestive linguistic and anthropological point having to do with sexual *inclusion*. I am taking my example from Father Paul Mankowski, S.J. Suppose you see a pictographic sign with a stick figure in a skirt. The figure is dropping litter. A red diagonal band cuts through the figure, in fact right through the skirt. We "read" it—with a hitch. What is the skirt doing there? What is the point?

Does the sign mean "No Littering by Women"? Everyone, feminists included, would furrow the brow and wonder whether the sign was meant in jest, or meant to offend. But if you see the pictograph of the "male" stick figure, straight up and down, no "hips," doing the same thing, you read it immediately: No Littering. No littering by anybody: by man, woman, or child. All are included, regardless of sex or age, in the single general figure.

Woman is to man as the specific is to the general. Human languages attest to it. Words for "mankind" commonly serve also for "adult male," or are based upon the word for "adult male," or reverse position with the word for "adult male," or have "adult male" as a secondary meaning. In English, "man" can mean either one, with hardly ever the slightest confusion. The dog is "man's best friend," we say, and everyone, even children, understands that *all human beings are comprehended in the one term*, which is simultaneously singular, all-inclusive, concrete, and personal. No word in English can do the same work. In German, the general "Mensch" is based upon "Mann," not upon "Frau," the word for woman, and indeed the indefinite pronoun meaning "somebody" or "everybody" is simply the word "Mann," unstressed: *man*. In Latin, the word *homo* meant *man* in the general sense; think of English *homicide*, which denotes the killing of a human being, simply. The word for adult male was *vir*. But speakers of Anglo-Saxon, contemporary with those Latin speakers, had the same words but with reversed senses: the word for human being in general was *wer*: a *werewolf* is half human being, half wolf. It doesn't have to be male. But one of the words for adult male, actually for a warrior, was *guma*, the cousin of Latin *homo*, which eventually became the modern English word *groom*. Greek *anthropos* meant human being, in its primary sense, but also *adult male*, secondarily. "A man had two sons," says Jesus at the beginning of his parable of the Prodigal Son (Luke 15:11). Nobody translates that as "a human being," yet it is Greek *anthropos*. You can find many such uses of *anthropos* in the New Testament, when the masculinity of the man is not stressed—as it is when the *men* (*andres*) lower the paralytic on his pallet through a hole they have made in the roof (Luke 5:18).

Today when women or girls enter a room full of their friends, they themselves will commonly say, "What are you guys doing?" They thus use a masculine term in a general sense, even while they have been trained to mangle their language when they write, lest it manifest the reality they cannot help but manifest in their common and relaxed speech. (In Newfoundland, by the way, the term is not *guys* but *b'ys*, that is, *boys*). A feminist may well give her daughter a masculine name, such as Ryan or Madison. Not even she will name her son Mary or Jennifer.

The masculine term is what is genuinely inclusive. Everything else is impersonal (*the human race*), abstract (*humanity*), vague and impersonal (*someone*), merely plural and not universal (*people*), possibly exclusive (*we*, as a substitute for *man*), or divisive, drawing a distinction where none is appropriate (*men and women*). We are all Adam. We are all meant to be Christ. Saint Paul could not have urged his brethren to put off the old *woman*—what on earth could that have meant to the centurion or the blacksmith or the youth in training? Everyone, men and women and children, both individually and all together, could immediately understand the command to put off the old *man*. We understand it right away, too. Even feminist basketball players use talk about "man-to-man" defense. We only pretend not to understand.

So if we call God by a feminine term, we suggest not universality but peculiarity—and circumscription.

The Causal Direction

I have already scouted the nonsense that Jesus said or did anything out of a craven submission to what the people around him

expected, and certainly no Christian dare insinuate that the Son of
God was just a man of his time. But the next move, not by a Christian,
is to say not that Jesus was a man of his time, but that he was a man,
simply, a human being and a male, and calling God "Father" was only
what such a creature would do. If we are not men, or if we choose not
to live in a patriarchal society, we may call God "Mother" if we please,
or not call God anything at all.

The objection begs a few questions. That is, it assumes from the
outset that there is nothing about God to be revealed by the term
"Father"—but that would imply that there is nothing about God to
be revealed by the term "Mother," either. It assumes that religion is a
mere creation of man, and not man's response to the self-revelation
of God; so that we are talking not about realities but about arbitrary
styles. What goes by the name of religion does not really possess what
we mean by that term; it does not possess its soul. Indeed such a thing
has no soul at all. This kind of "religion" is an accessory to your life,
like a sailboat or a new suit. The objection also assumes that "Father"
is merely metaphorical, and not a name. Since no metaphor can capture the whole reality of anything, any one metaphor must always be
complemented by others, and thus "Mother" is thought to add some
information about God that "Father" does not convey.

Let us proceed with care here.

First, ours is the least patriarchal society in the history of the
world, if only because we have the wealth to allow us to skate for a
while on our past successes. We can "afford" to experiment in unre-
ality, just as the rich man can afford to sow thistles on his farmland
and see if he can grind them up to bake bread. But no other form of
society actually works for man. Patriarchy is built into our nature.
Wherever the rule by fathers is at ebb, liberty languishes, because the
engines of government must come in to deal with the chaos that
always results. In fact, as I have said and as can be demonstrated

abundantly by the history of the modern nation, government grows, and grows more intrusive and bloated and ineffectual, by the fading of the fathers.

We may ask then whether a patriarchal creature will naturally look upon God as Father. The answer is not easy. All peoples have had some father-god or chief of the deities to look to: Odin, Zeus, Osiris, Ahura-Mazda, Brahma. But most peoples have also had their goddesses too. Sometimes these are gentle and wise, like Isis, but often they are brutal and bloodthirsty, such as the Sumerian sea-goddess Tiamat, from whose dismembered limbs the triumphant Marduk created the world. In *Till We Have Faces*, C. S. Lewis imagines a pre-Christian people worshiping a fertility goddess called Ungit, hideous, more of a thing than a person, fearsome and malevolent and holy, demanding sacrifice of blood, because you do not get from the earth what you do not first put into it. Lewis was quite aware of Mediterranean goddess-worship. Womb and tomb go together.

So the Jews were unusual, I might say unique, in *not having a goddess*: not a hint of one, not a shadow of a memory of one. Likewise they were unusual in *not having priestesses*. In none of the diverse cultures of the Mediterranean, and in no culture that I know about, were women the chief links between the human and the divine, and the reality falls far short of what any feminist would want as an alternative to patriarchal worship, but it is difficult to think of any religion besides Judaism that is without priestesses of some kind. The sibyl at Delphi inhaled the psychotropic fumes of burning laurel leaves and of the gases coming up from the volcanic rocks where the oracle was stationed; it was not a job you sought for its pleasure. Virgil describes the inspiration of the Sibyl in the *Aeneid* as a kind of rape by the god Apollo. Rome had her Vestal virgins, who dared not think of betraying their virginity if they wanted to preserve their lives, and the Canaanites had their temple prostitutes, women and boys. It is also absurd to say that the Jews were contemptuous of women, who play a far greater and more significant part in their sacred history than women do in Greece and Rome and Carthage and Babylon. We need only think of Sarah, Rebecca, and Rachel, or of the judge Deborah, or Jael with her hammer and tent-peg, or of Ruth, the loyal woman of Moab and the great-grandmother of King David, or of Esther, the savior of her people in Persia. The Jewish mother was always a force to be reckoned with.

When Jesus called God "Father," he was not indulging in a metaphor, but using a name and commanding his followers to use it in turn. It is not that he called God "Father" because God was rather like a human father. The fatherhood of God is primary. Human fatherhood is derivative and secondary. Human fathers reflect, in a shadowy and sin-distorted way, the essential and all-encompassing fatherhood of God. This is, of course, as Jesus and the evangelists and Saint Paul and everyone else in the Church saw it and preached it.

Here words necessarily fail us, because whenever we predicate anything about God, we run the risk of circumscribing him, so that it is easier and more secure to take the *via negativa* and say what God is *not*: he is not mortal, he is not finite, he is not ever mistaken, and so forth. Still, the assertion is that God is Father, and we must at least begin to ask what that means.

Creation, Not Procreation

Suppose we were to say that the relation of God to the universe is that of a *mother* to her child. We would immediately find ourselves in trouble, because the mother brings forth life from her own substance, from her body; and this would be so especially if we supposed that she could do so at will and without being acted upon by a father. That would imply an identity of being between her and her offspring:

what comes from the mother is like the mother, or is but the mother in other forms. The ancient Roman philosophers noted the connection between the substance of the mother and her child, and, using a bit of folk etymology, said that was why the words *mater, mother,* and *materia, matter,* were so alike. Matter is the mother: the mother is material.

Hence it is a short step from calling God "mother" to raising the material universe to the level of the greatest god. That is, if you see God as "mother," soon will you see the material universe as a god. You will worship the goddess Gaia, the Earth Mother. But there are problems with that. If the earth is a mother, she seems to be a very bad one—the kind who does not care for the welfare of her offspring. She swallows them up. You cannot escape the bloody cycle of birth and maturity and procreation and age and death. That is all there is. Earth of herself offers no more. The material universe of itself offers no more.

The tremendous revelation to the ancient Hebrews—who show no particular sign of theological genius that would cause us to think they had come up with it on their own—was that God was not like that. "In the beginning," says that quiet and utterly shattering first sentence of Genesis, "God created the heavens and the earth." There was nothing, and then there was creation. God, who is absolute being, imparts being. He goes out of himself, as it were. He makes what is not God. The whole universe—the heavens and the earth—is not God. It is not a necessary birthing from God. It need not have been. Creation from nothing is deliberate agency. It is the ultimate arrow.

That explains why the Hebrews were forbidden to make "a graven image, or any likeness of anything that is in heaven above, or that is in the earth beneath, or that is in the water under the earth" (Exodus 20:4). The prohibition did not forbid the Hebrews to be artists for their own pleasure; such artists did not exist at the time. It meant that they were never to confound God with creation. The Hebrews who made their graven image of the golden calf while Moses was atop Mount Sinai fell into that confusion: "These are your gods, O Israel," they cried, "who brought you up out of the land of Egypt!" (Exodus 32:4). That is not so much to make a mistake about God as to misunderstand him utterly.

We also run the risk of domesticating God, of turning him into a creature we can comprehend and, given certain rules of religious behavior, control. The mother gives birth to the baby, and there they are, the mother suckling the child—a breathtakingly beautiful image, and good and true, but at best a quite narrow image for grasping God's relation to the world, and at worst a distortion. "He's not tame," says C. S. Lewis's Mr. Beaver of happy memory, referring to Aslan the Lion, "but he's good." "Were you there," thunders God out of the whirlwind to the suffering and self-justifying Job, "when I laid the foundation of the earth? Tell me, if you have understanding!" (Job 38:4). He does not lay a hand on Job's shoulder to give him a little poetry with some opium in it, to make him feel good about himself. Over and over again in the Old Testament we are warned that we dare not pretend to tell what God will do. God comforts; he also warns, reproves, and punishes; and that is still his love acting, good but not tame, and better because not tame. When Jeremiah said that the Lord would lay waste to Jerusalem and the temple, "the priests and the prophets and all the people laid hold of the prophet, saying 'You shall die! Why have you prophesied in the name of the Lord, saying, "This house shall be like Shiloh, and this city shall be desolate, without inhabitant?"'" (Jeremiah 26:8–9). They thought they had God by a collar and a leash. Or, to put it another way, they relied upon what they thought they knew about God, rather than upon *the truth*.

The deity who does what we want because it has cuddly feelings about us and would never want us to feel bad is an invention of our weakling time. Such a deity could never have created the tiger or the leviathan of the deep. But God *has* created this world, a dangerous and an adventurous world, in which real things happen, with glorious and terrible consequences. It is not a birth from a womb, but a creation of his mind and will and power; he might have created, and somewhere perhaps has created, an entirely different universe. No one dare set bounds to the divine artist, who is bound only to his infinitely powerful, infinitely wise, and infinitely good self. Not tame.

The Corn of Wheat

It appears from the experience of the Western churches that when a liturgy is feminized, the attention is turned from the vertical to the horizontal, and people look to one another rather than to God. They look also for moral approval, for social sanction. They want to be assured that they are good, after all. They hear sermons that tell them to do the things they already do, but that never tell them to cease committing their most cherished sins. Awe is gone.

I am not entirely sure why women and men in our time have permitted it to be so. My reading of the women mystics of the past suggests that they did know and cherish that awe before the power and glory of God. "I am he who is," says Christ to Catherine of Siena in a vision, "and you are she who is not."[1] It is hard to imagine a bolder expression of the infinite distance between the creature and the Creator than that. Teresa of Avila, who is most womanly in her desire for spiritual betrothal to Christ, is also womanly, and decidedly not feminist, in calling God "his Majesty" and urging upon her sisters such progress in the interior life that they will reach the inmost mansion, the seventh, where "so extreme is her longing for the will of God to be done in her that whatever His Majesty does she considers to be for the best: if He wills that she should suffer, well and good; if not, she does not worry herself to death as she did before."[2]

Perhaps suffering is the key. The good woman does not want her small child to suffer. She is right about that. Babies should be kept safe. But the good man does want his child to suffer, if we understand the word correctly. I am not just talking here about the man's insistence upon the law and putting teeth into it. "Except a corn of wheat shall fall into the ground and die," says Jesus, "it abideth alone" (John 12:24). Even if we were not sinners, something analogous to suffering must occur as the creature develops from one stage to another. The grown person must put away the things of the child. The chick breaks out of the shell. The achievement of a worthy end must involve sweat and blood. There is no comfortable way to travel to a new land. You cannot dig a good hole without thrusting the shovel and sometimes leaning all your weight on it to pry up a stone. Thomas Edison used to catch a couple of hours of sleep at night by lying down on a table in his laboratory. Soldiers that do not drill cease to be soldiers. They become easy marks for the enemy, to fertilize their fields. Conquest requires the fight, and the fight cannot be undertaken by the self-indulgent. And we are sinners to boot, foolish, self-willed, and sullen. If we are not compelled to suffer, we will remain moral toddlers all our lives.

I have long heard it said that if men bore children, they would not be so eager to prohibit abortion. Of course, if men bore children, they would be women and not men, but the implication is that men are notably easy on themselves and hard on women. Hence the so-called "double standard" regarding sexual morality: women are or were held to the severe ideal of chastity, while men can visit houses of ill repute and not lose by it—the "ill repute" applies only to the women. To which I have two answers. First, though the moral law applies equally to both, for the sheer pragmatism of it, the arithmetic of it, you gain much more by expecting women to be continent and chaste than by expecting chastity of men. If almost all of your women are chaste, it will not matter, practically, whether a quarter or half or almost all of your men are so; basically, your children will be born within wedlock. But if almost all of your men are chaste, but your women are not, you will be overrun with illegitimate children. The women are the gatekeepers.

But second, it simply *is not true that men are harder on women than they are on themselves, in general.* Sex is the great exception that proves the rule. In every other matter, men are if anything prone to allow women to do what they would never allow men to do. The woman may run away from danger. The man who does so will be despised. The woman may break down in tears when she hears terrible news, making it impossible for something urgent to get done. The man must deny himself the comfort of those tears. The woman may appeal to fear to absolve herself from a promise. The man may not make that appeal. You can call a man an idiot to his face, and if he hates you for it, people may think even the less of him for not being able to take criticism. Call a woman an idiot to her face—well, decent men do not do that. The high school linebacker mouths off to his coach. The coach decks him, and everybody on the team will side with the coach, and so will the linebacker, when he grows up. Consider what it would mean if women treated women who procure abortions as men treat men who desert their troops in time of war, or as men treated men who stole horses in the Old West. Too harsh? Were it not so, you might as well surrender your land as soon as the enemy attacks. Were it not so, forget about settling the West.

The Jesus who brings comfort is the same Jesus who brings suffering: "If any man would come after me, let him deny himself and take up his cross and follow me. For whoever would save his life will lose it, and whoever loses his life for my sake will find it" (Matthew

16:24–25). That is the ultimate in suffering: to die, or to live a life that is also a continual dying. "I have been crucified with Christ," says Saint Paul, with considerable asperity, to the Galatians, and when he begs them to treat one another with kindness and patience, he says also that "those who belong to Christ Jesus have crucified the flesh with its passions and desires" (Galatians 2:20, 5:24). The author of the letter to the Hebrews suggests that the obedience of the Son to the Father was made perfect in suffering (Hebrews 5:8). This is not hatred of life. It is a bold affirmation of life, in its rejection of a comfort that dulls and stifles.

That is how we should understand the *askesis* practiced by both men and women in the Church when it was led by the manly. The Greek ascetic is engaged in military drill or in preparation for athletic competition. He is in training. That, too, is the meaning behind the Latin word *exercitus*, *army*, from which we derive the word *exercise*. If we think it bizarre that a Saint Anthony should retire to a disused fort in the Egyptian desert for twenty years and not see the face of another human being, perhaps we should note the results of this severe training: Anthony became the chief of a movement that swept through the Christian world, attracting many disciples in his own lifetime, and became the founder of Christian monasticism. And he did so without growing morose. Quite the contrary, he was an amiable and valorous man, and I think it is no coincidence that a person of such extraordinary spiritual discipline and strength should live to the age of 106.

Can men understand what passion, what eager embrace of suffering, could move Anthony to do what he did? Consider the men who march back and forth, without casting a single glance to the side, without a smile, nor even a motion of the hand to swat a fly, at the Tomb of the Unknown Soldier in Arlington National Cemetery. That is what men do when they want to make what is sacred present to themselves and to others. I am reminded of what an older altar boy did one day when a well-meaning woman had placed a cushion for him and his younger fellows to kneel on, rather than on the hard stone floor. As he passed it at the beginning of the service he bent down without breaking stride, snatched it up, and flung it sideways into the vestry. Men and boys do not always like what is comforting. How can we build up our strength unless by suffering?

And what is holy is never something that we can merely adopt as our own. We must bow down to it and pray to be taken up into it. The holy is not ours, but we want to belong to the holy. A manly religion acknowledges what is sacred, what is not to be touched with profane hands, and in the light of that respect for sacred space, women and men both can flourish; but an effeminate religion loses the sense of the sacred, will not discipline itself, flees from suffering, grows flabby and sickly, and then dies. It is no great triumph for women that a female pastor should preside over a corpse.

Households Ordered to the Glory of God

Perhaps we may say this: Since we are embodied souls, and since the union of man and woman in marriage is indeed a great mystery, figuring forth the marriage of Christ and the Church, any disorder between the sexes will be mirrored in a disorder between man and God. No order in the household, no order in the soul, no order in the Church. Worship will not then be more *feminine* (as in such Catholic devotions as the May crowning and praying the rosary) but rather *effeminate* (holding your neighbor's sweaty hand while you say the Our Father at Mass; turning the altar boys from knights of the faith in training into the very occasional girly kid in pajamas, or a boy suffering the command to serve but smoldering as he does it; turning the music into a kindergarten happy-time to celebrate our own wonderfulness). The manly Church of Saint Ignatius and the early Jesuits, fighters for the faith, from whose determination the English word mission derives, produced also the most womanly Saint Teresa; the manly Church of the Crusaders built all across Europe the cathedrals that the astute Henry Adams called jewel-boxes presented to Mary. Manliness and womanliness go hand in hand, as Adam and Eve did before they fell. Effeminacy and machismo also—as allies in disaffection and destruction, because they hardly love one another.

Again we may note the order. If the man clears the earth, the woman can grow her garden. If the liturgy is governed by a manly and soldierly submission to the glory of God, then the church flourishes, and there is free room for the womanly to take root in innumerable ways. But if the liturgy is rendered effeminate by a priest who shies away from masculine camaraderie and risk-taking, or by a mannish woman who perceives everyone with a deep voice as a threat to her authority—if the attention is taken from the transcendent God, the creator of heaven and earth, and turned mainly toward our feelings for one another, calling "love" what is really expediency and a shrug, then the church empties. The men lose interest. The boys never catch the interest at all. The girls bristle under the watch of the older women, and they also leave, because boys are a lot more exciting than old ladies are. There simply is no place for the manly and the womanly, because the land is left untended, the weeds and brambles grow up, the shingles fall off the roof, and the building is sold to a man as a storage bin for auto parts, or to a woman as a shop for dressing hair.

Begin and end with worship of God not for what he does for us, but for who he is in himself—his ineffable glory. Then we can understand him as the love, as Dante says, "that moves the sun and the other stars," a love that dwelt in himself and was himself before he created the world. It is a deepening of our understanding of glory to see that it is also love. Says Robert Browning's medical man Karshish, after having met his first follower of Christ, that same Lazarus who was raised from the dead:

> The very God! think, Abib; dost thou think?
> So, the All-Great, were the All-Loving too—
> So, through the thunder comes a human voice
> Saying, "O heart I made, a heart beats here!
> Face, my hands fashioned, see it in myself!
> Thou hast no power nor mayst conceive of mine,
> But love I gave thee, with myself to love,
> And thou must love me who have died for thee! (304–12)

But no one would say, "Just think—the all-loving is, wait a bit, also *almighty*!" No—that direction does not work. And if our idea of God is all love and no awe, we end up instead with the idol of what is called "moral therapeutic deism," a deity of comfort, a universal cuddle, a hug and a kiss as the old lady says to the sinner, "Oh, sonny, don't worry about it. You gave it a try."

It is thus men who guard the holy, and in our time that means also the very idea of the holy. They are like Moses with the tablets etched in fire. They are like Daniel, who would rather be thrown to the lions than bow before the idol of Nebuchadnezzar. They are like Thomas Becket, slain at the altar because he would not permit King Henry II to lay his secular hands on ecclesiastical law. When men thus lead, women follow, and often with a self-denying enthusiasm that puts the men to shame: think of Joan of Arc at the stake.

Ultimately the attack upon the home, and upon the marriage of man and woman, is an attack on the God who made man and woman. And the return to sanity and decency, and to genuine gratitude of each sex for the other, is one step, but a large step, toward saying, with the lad who had wandered into a far country and squandered his inheritance, "I shall arise, and go to my father" (Luke 15:18).

Notes

Chapter One: Strength

1. Except whether otherwise noted, Bible passages quoted throughout the book are taken from the King James Version.
2. New International Version.
3. Except where a note indicates otherwise, the translations throughout the book are mine.

Chapter Two: Agency

1. Larry R. Vandevert, "The Appearance of the Child Prodigy 10,000 Years Ago: An Evolutionary and Developmental Explanation," *Journal of Mind & Behavior* 30, no. 1 (December 2009): 15–32.

Chapter Five: The Vision

1. Edith Hamilton and Huntington Cairns, eds., *Plato: The Collected Dialogues* (Princeton, 1961).
2. Flannery O'Connor, "Greenleaf," in *The Complete Short Stories* (New York: Farrar, Straus, and Giroux, 1978), 317.
3. Margery Kempe, *The Book of Margery Kempe*, trans. B. A. Windeatt (London: Penguin, 1985), 179.
4. Plotinus, *The Six Enneads*, trans. Stephen MacKenna (London: P. L. Warner, 1917).
5. Lao-Tzu, *Tao Te Ching*, trans. James Legge (1891), chapter 25.

6. Pseudo-Dionysius, *The Divine Names* in *The Complete Works*, trans. Colm Luibheid (Mahwah, New Jersey: Paulist Press, 1987), 54.

Chapter Six: The Father in Heaven

1. See Catherine of Siena, *The Dialogue of Catherine of Siena*, trans. Algar Thogold (London: Kegan, Paul, 1907).
2. Teresa of Avila, *The Interior Castle*, trans. E. Allison Peers (Bottom of the Hill Publishing, 1999), 173–74.

Index

A

activity (as a masculine characteristic), 10, 29, 31, 40, 58, 63, 65, 101, 162

Adam (biblical), vii–viii, 31, 146–47, 171, 182

Aeneas, 16–17

Aeschylus, 128–29

Agamemnon, 128

agency, 162, 175

Alekhine, Alexander, 55

apostles (twelve biblical), 92–94, 159, 161

aqueducts, 32–40, 45

Aquinas, Thomas, 60, 134–35

Argos ("Flash"), 18–19

Atwood, Margaret, 41

B

Barnard, Charles, 35–38

Battle of Maldon, The, (poem), 21

Beatrice, 23, 103, 131, 148, 159

Beauvoir, Simone de, 121

Brother Karamazov, The, 166, 168

brotherhood, 68, 71, 90, 92–93, 161–63

Browning, Robert, 183

C

camaraderie, 40, 66, 87, 182

Catholicism, 87, 181

Cheney, John Vance, 47

Chesterton, G. K., 119–20, 136

Cicero, 122

Clinton, Hillary, 120

Clytemnestra, 128

Colonial Pipeline, 39–40, 42

Conal (hero of Irish mythology), 67

Constitution, U.S., 80, 88

Council of Nicaea, 136

Crenshaw, Kimberlé Williams, 40

Croton Aqueduct, 35, 38–39, 45

D

da Vinci, Leonardo, 50

Dante, 23–24, 56, 103, 131, 148, 151, 153, 158–59, 182

David (biblical), 48, 108–9, 174

Desdemona, 13, 144

Dickens, Charles, 85, 118

Dido, 16

differences between men and women

  behavioral differences, 10–11, 24, 54, 135, 143, 151–54, 158

  natural vs. learned differences, 11–12, 14–21, 30, 61–62

  physical differences, viii, x, 2–3, 5–11

Dostoyevsky, Fyodor, 166

dynamic enmity, 87, 94, 168

E

Edison, Thomas, 54, 116, 178

education, 46, 90, 98, 110–11, 115–17, 142

  boys in school, xii, 41–42, 46–47, 55

Engels, Friedrich, 111

Enkidu, 67–68, 71

envy, 100–101

equality, viii, 42, 71–72, 74–76, 79, 87, 93, 102, 162–63

Eumaeus, 18–19

Eve (biblical), viii, 31, 146–47, 182

F

family, the, 71, 101, 111, 114, 121–22, 125, 129–30, 134, 163

  breakdown of the family, 40–41, 96, 101, 105, 112, 121, 124–25

fatherhood, 103–5, 107–9, 163, 174

feminists, xi, 11, 24, 30–31, 40, 44, 61, 81, 83, 94–95, 100–102, 143, 164, 167–68, 170–71, 173, 177

Fermat's Last Theorem, 50
Fermat, Pierre de, 50–51
freedom of association, 88
Friedan, Betty, 121
Furies, the, 128–29

G
Gauss, Carl Friedrich, 156–57
Gilder, George, 25
Gilgamesh, 67–68, 71
Gladstone, William, 84
God, vii, 31, 48–49, 56, 60, 62,
    78, 92, 94, 100, 109, 115, 132,
    136–37, 146, 148–49, 152–54,
    159, 164–66, 169, 171–77,
    181–83
government, 39, 75, 79–80,
    82–85, 102, 119–20, 140–41,
    163, 172–73
Great Expectations (Dickens),
    118
Grimm, Jacob, 52–53
Grimm's Law, 52–53

H
Hebrews, 175–76, 180
Hemon, Louis, 27

hierarchy, viii, 31, 71–79, 84, 87,
    93, 137, 162–63, 165
Homer, 18, 86
homeschooling, 117
hope, 43, 105, 109–10, 122, 165
household, viii, 13, 19, 43–44,
    84–85, 113, 118, 167, 181

I
Industrial Revolution, 120
infrastructure, 42–43
intersectionality, 39–40, 43

J
James, Bill, 53–54
Jesus Christ, 91–93, 108–9, 152,
    159, 161, 164–66, 169–72, 174,
    178–80
John, Saint (apostle), 91, 93, 137,
    159, 166, 178
Joseph, Saint (father of Jesus),
    93, 108–9

K
Kant, Immanuel, 135
Kempe, Margery, 152–53, 158
Klakherrit (Native American
    character), 20

L

La Vita nuova (Dante), 56, 131
labor. *See* work
Leahy, Donnell, 116
Lewis, C. S., 102, 115, 173, 176
linguistics, 52, 169
Lucas, Jerry, 54–55

M

machines, ix, 30, 37, 51, 59, 65,
　　72, 112, 119, 138, 143, 163
MacMaster, Natalie, 116
male domination, 101–2
Mandeville, John, 110
manhood, xi–xii, 1–2, 16, 83,
　　102, 105, 145, 165
Mankowski, Father Paul, S.J.,
　　169
manliness, vii, xii, 182
Marbury vs. Madison, 80
Marcel, Gabriel, 105–7
marriage, xii, 66, 110, 114,
　　125–26, 149, 181, 183
Marx, Karl, 111, 156
masculinity, 123, 133, 171
　　"toxic masculinity," xii–xiii,
　　44
Michelangelo, 89–90, 116, 159

Milton, John, vii–viii, 31, 56–57,
　　108, 146, 163
motherhood, 24, 106–7, 127, 129,
　　133, 172, 174–76
　　single mothers, 96–97, 112
Mozart, 55, 135
Museum of Industry (Nova
　　Scotia), 41

N

New York City, 35
Newton, Isaac, 157

O

O'Connor, Flannery, 152
Odysseus, 13, 17–19
Oisin (hero of Irish mythology),
　　20
Oresteia (Aeschylus), 128
Orestes, 128–29
Othello, 144

P

patriarchy, 12, 101–2, 104, 107,
　　109, 114, 121, 130, 172–73
Paul, Saint, 1, 22–23, 112, 155, 163,
　　171, 174, 180
Peguy, Charles, 105–6

Peter, Saint (apostle), 23, 92–94, 159, 164

Phaedrus, 150–51

Pissarro, Camille, 149

politics, xii, 9, 61, 83, 85, 94–95, 97, 106, 142, 164

    women in politics, 83, 95–98

Poultry Market, The (painting), 149

Putnam, Robert, 123

R

rage to master, the, 54, 59

religion, 44, 85, 172–73, 176, 181

Renaissance, the, 89

Rensselaer, Mariana Griswold van, 83–85, 142

Roman Empire, 16, 19, 31, 34, 85, 100, 173–74

S

sabermetrics, 54

safe spaces, 22, 103

Sartre, Jean-Paul, 121

Sawyer, Tom, 68–69

sexism, 44–45

Shakespeare, William, 56–57, 75–76, 100, 108, 143

skills, 12, 33, 40–43, 45–46, 74, 81, 165–66

Socrates, 151

Sons of Mor (Irish folktale), 66

Spenser, Edmund, 148–49

suffering, 18, 178–81

Supreme Court, the U.S., 80–81

T

Tarkington, Booth, 144

team, the, 5, 63–64, 66, 70–75, 77, 82–83, 86–87, 90, 93–94, 161–63, 165, 167, 179

Tempest, The (Shakespeare), 75, 79, 148

Teresa of Avila, Saint, 153–54, 177, 182

theories, 155–57

Tiber River, 31

transgender movement, 2

Twain, Mark, 69

V

Vandervert, Larry R., 58

virility, 1

vision, 131–32, 135–37, 143, 150–51, 154, 164–66

Volstead Act, 139–40

W

Wanderer, The, (poem), 21

Washington, Booker T., 42

Wiles, Andrew, 51–52

Winner, Ellen, 54–55

women's suffrage movement,
     83–85, 139

Woolf, Virginia, 57

work, x, 3–10, 12, 24, 27–29, 31,
     34, 37–38, 41–46, 51, 54, 57–58,
     64, 72, 74, 79, 82–85, 89, 98,
     105, 107, 113, 115, 123, 135, 139,
     141–43, 145, 148, 161
     women in the workforce,
          43–44, 84